Women Married to Men in Ministry

D1569968

Women Married to Men in Ministry

Breaking the Sound Barrier Together

TERESA FLINT-BORDEN
WITH BARBARA COOPER

Abingdon Press
Nashville

WOMEN MARRIED TO MEN IN MINISTRY
BREAKING THE SOUND BARRIER TOGETHER

LIBRARY OF CONGRESS CATALOGING-IN-PUBLICATION DATA

Flint-Borden, Teresa,
    Women married to men in ministry : breaking the sound barrier together / Teresa Flint-Borden ; with Barbara Cooper.
    p. cm.
    Companion to: Hit the bullseye and Direct hit.
    Includes bibliographical references.
    ISBN 978-0-687-49185-8 (pbk. : alk. paper)
    1. Spouses of clergy. I. Cooper, Barbara, 1923– II. Title.

    BV4395.F55 2007
    253'.22—dc22

                                     2007027478

07 08 09 10 11 12 13 14 15 16—10 9 8 7 6 5 4 3 2 1

MANUFACTURED IN THE UNITED STATES OF AMERICA

To a man who has both vision and courage. A leader who accepts the mission and implements changes to transform Growing Healthy Churches worldwide—my husband, Paul Borden. Thank you for your support throughout this project.

To all the courageous Women Married to Men in Ministry and women in ministry and their spouses for their tremendous sacrifice in breaking the sound barrier. You are on the front lines of the battle, transforming one church at a time into Great Commission Churches.

To my firstborn child, my daughter, Leah-LaShelle, who is the most integrous woman I know, a woman of justice, a trait beginning in childhood. She has a belief that her mom can do anything—even write this book! And to her son, my grandson, Wren, who said, "Grandma! Just think how good you'll feel when it's all done!"

To my only son, Cory—your love and life were inspirational. Thanks for being my biggest fan.

To my dear grandmother, my mentor, who led me to the knowledge of Jesus; what a journey it is!

CONTENTS

JUST BECOMING OURSELVES

One theme woven throughout *Women Married to Men in Ministry* is that the transformer cannot stand apart from the transformation. All of us struggle with transitioning through change, even if that change takes us up the denominational leadership ladder. Even me.

After all the notoriety and successes I have experienced in my own career, I now find I don't even have a "real" job. Being a woman married to an Executive Minister is a nonjob, a place without definition. Perhaps it's become too defined by my husband's position, which makes my "role" an unresourced place of invisibility and isolation—one of knowing about so many people and yet not knowing anyone. Still, I see, hear, and observe the change process and detect and experience so much pain and dysfunction within the body of Christ.

I have always had a direction, but now at sixty-plus, my only son has died. This child of my heart is gone after four treacherous years of battling AIDS. Then I left my firstborn, my darling daughter, far away in Denver, struggling to keep her sixteen-year-old son safe from a life of drugs and family dysfunction. This feels as if I have been hit in the back of the knees and in the stomach at the same time—left in a fetal position. In addition, I had two major surgeries, and I moved across the country to a different state, leaving my business of twenty years, my contacts, my friendships, my network, and the dream home that we had just built.

Going through menopause, I sometimes cannot sleep. I wake up at 1:00, 3:00, 5:00 a.m., my thoughts and heart racing. What will I do with the rest of my life? For me it is like being in outer space, drifting away into this dark, void place with what I thought was my identity now obliterated.

And questions—deep God questions: What does it mean when your faith and your experience come crashing into each other? What is the purpose? What do I really need to learn from this experience? Where do I fit in God's plan? What do I really want to do with the time that I have left? What will make me feel alive again? What will make me feel like my being here mattered? Will the echo of my voice be heard, or will it return to me unanswered? Who am I? Who are you? Do you know? How do we find out? Where do we go? When do we go? How do we get there? What transportation vehicle will get us there?

I do have the opportunity to form something myself, and shift from *what* I supposedly must *be*, to *whom* I believe I want to *become*. So, I am using the platform of this position as a runway for serving Women Married to Men in Ministry, embarking upon systemic change within the church by writing this book. I started a nonprofit corporation that benefits women. I help women who are starting over. I endeavor to be an encouragement to Women Married to Men in Ministry within our region. I am particularly concerned for our Hispanic sisters but certainly only scratching the very surface of that need. I have some blips on my radar screen to do something more about women's needs—perhaps a day spa retreat center—the flight plan is not yet filed. I will continue on my journey above and beyond with God's help.

Postscript

I really struggled with this self-disclosure, as I am a private person, having experienced broken trust in the past, but it is my truth. Living as a Woman Married to a Man in Ministry through this systemic change process, it strikes me that a big part of the pain and suffering comes from not being able to voice our truth and have it heard and responded to in a safe place. So, many deep breaths and much agonizing later, I am saying it out loud for both safe and unsafe people to read. This book is about courage and risk; I find I must walk my talk. My hope and prayer is that you will find a safe person and way to express your deepest truths, breaking the cycle of lonely isolation that we have been living in, allowing us to live healthy, whole lives in our service to God, spouse, family, church, and world.

ACKNOWLEDGMENTS

To all the women in Scripture who dared—in voice and in action. Who still teach us how to find wings on which to fly today.

To all the women and men who contributed their stories. You are breaking the sound barrier. You know who you are. God bless you!

Teresa Flint-Borden:
To Dorothy, my friend and faithful typist, and her pastor husband, Bud, for input and insights.

To Brad, futurist, master wordsmith, miracle-working project manager, out-of-this-world crazy-genius sidekick, and newfound friend—Thank you. Without you, this book would not be possible.

To Barbara, my collaborating writer, and now cut-and-paste expert, professional counselor, ordained minister, and Woman Married to a Man in Ministry who serves as a copilot. Thank you for the role you play in my life as a trusted friend and ally, for allowing me to be a part of your amazing and courageous life. You are indeed breaking the sound barrier; thank you for your commitment to this project. Without your deep insights, this book would not be a reality today.

To Kelli, Luke, Em, Meg, and Tess; Jeff, Keena, and Addison.

To Connie, Linda, Cathy, Joan, Susan, Tami, Rita, Barbara, Edie, Laura, Nadean, and José—Thank you for your encouragement and belief in me.

To everyone on our team from Abingdon Press, especially Paul Franklyn, John Kutsko, and Kathy Armistead.

Barbara Cooper:
To Gary, my partner in love and life, and my true copilot in ministry. Your courageous and egalitarian spirit inspires me to soar beyond the sound barrier to realize the fullness of God's call upon my life. I am forever grateful.

Great Commission Flights: Women in Ministries of Transformation

*Go therefore and make disciples of all nations, baptizing them in
the name of the Father and of the Son and of the Holy Spirit, and
teaching them to obey everything that I have commanded you.
And remember, I am with you always, to the end of the age.*
THE "GREAT COMMISSION," MATTHEW 28:19-20

Life in Christ is supposed to be about transformation, and God calls
leaders to equip his followers for that process. No one said that
being a ministry leader would be easy. But the ultimate eternal
rewards are worth it, as we participate in helping congregations experience healthy change. Sometimes, though, despite sincere intentions and
diligent preparations, we end up on unexpected journeys where our best
dreams temporarily morph into our worst nightmares.

Great Commission Hijacked!

You've long anticipated this new and exciting adventure. It's what you
readied yourself for, and so many people say it's worth the journey. So, you
board a plane named *Great Commission*. You're going to a part of the
world you've never seen. Surely, it'll be an amazing trip with scenic
panoramas of God's good creation. More important, your flight will take
you to communities you've never been able to go to before. Think of

meeting all these new people and introducing them to the maker of Heaven and Earth, and eventually hearing his words, "Well done, good and faithful servant!"

You and your whole group board the plane, buckle up, and wait for takeoff. Now airborne, you look out the window; you enjoy crossing the Grand Canyon. Everyone is in awe of its magnificence and beauty! As you enjoy the view from above, you smile to yourself. For the first time, you realize the depth and breadth of the great chasm. As beautiful as it is from this angle, it would be a steep, long, and difficult hike. Suddenly you find yourself wishing you were in better shape.

Breaking this tranquillity, you hear murmurings somewhere in the background. Where is this coming from? Now, oddly, the atmosphere seems different, stale. Foreboding closes in on you, and you're not sure why. Everything around appears normal, but somehow your intuition tells you it isn't. Something is off-kilter.

Suddenly, three people from your group are making their way to the front of the plane. What's the problem? Why the loud commotion?

You keep waiting for an announcement. But nothing comes.

Then there's an explosion. The cockpit door flies open. Shouts erupt!

The pilots—something is happening to the pilots!

The passenger beside you muffles a faint cry.

Panic and turbulence. The plane begins to lose altitude.

"Stay in your seat!"

Then the realization stabs you, "We're being hijacked."

Now one hijacker yells, "Get your heads down!"

Another screams directly at you, "Shut up, or else!"

You feel the plane bank and turn. Your temples are pounding. Your stomach tightens. Your hands go cold. Your brain is hyperalert and numb simultaneously. You're disoriented and shaky.

A hijacker forces the pilot and copilot into the cabin. *My God, they're bound and gagged! Who is flying this plane? Where are they taking us?*

Horrific as being hijacked is, now something worse—a few seats back, a cluster of people from your own group begin negotiating with the hijackers! Why are they doing that?

Hey, those people are my friends. They signed on to take the trip with me. What is that they're saying? They can't really mean it. Why are they so ready to turn over everything and everyone else for the sake of their own safety and security? *Traitors!*

What's happening? Will I ever get out of this alive? I never thought this would happen to me.

A moment of calm and clarity dawns. Yes, you'll risk it. Cautiously and quietly, you sneak out your cell phone and dial for help. You whisper key facts to the operator.

Just then, a voice (the flight attendant?) overrides the roar of the engine: "We're takin' this plane down for refueling!"

But, you are hearing the landing gear move into place. *We're landing now?*

You find pen and paper, scribble a note. You write on the front "Pass this around." Then start it on its way with a prayer, hoping it doesn't fall into the wrong hands. And now you wait and pray some more.

More commotion. They're untying the pilot. Why are they doing that?

Another announcement: "Get ready for a crash landing. Cross your arms. Put them on the headrest in front of you! Get your heads down."

Years pass in a matter of minutes.

With a stunning thud, the plane slams down. As it bounces, your body slams forward.

Brakes screech and squeal, throwing you back.

It's now or never to make your move, regardless how many people go with you. "*Move out! Now!*"

You bolt forward, as do others. With great urgency, you mass forward. There is more shouting. But as fearful as you are, you keep moving forward.

The hijackers are in view.

Overwhelmed, but still with great struggle, the usurpers are subdued.

But, there is a cost. There is always a cost.

It's over.

Relieved but still shaken, exhausted and strangely sad, you gaze around. Some of your friends scatter and run. Were they the ones talking to the hijackers?

Mumbling a quick prayer, you sigh deeply. The journey isn't over. *We're not even halfway there. I'm not sure I want to get back on a plane— ever. But there are people waiting for me, depending on me. My God, traveling is never going to be the same. Am I always going to be afraid that this will happen again?*

But the next leg of the trip will be different; it will have to be. You won't finish this journey with those who started with you. Lives were saved, even while some relationships were lost. Even so, the cost was great.

Can I ever board a plane again?

Around you, grim faces give way to relief and hope. There are some tears and even a few whoops. Sure, there is fear and trepidation; yet, there is also renewed determination. You once were lost, but now are found.

Buckle up. Time for takeoff. Take a deep breath. You can do this!

What was on the note? What saved the day? What unites and emboldens a group of travelers? What allows them to be courageous enough to regain control, returning to the original flight plan of the Great Commission?

Shifting from an Unpaved Road to Finding Myself in Orbit

In the late 1990s, I became immersed in the complex challenges of transition for "turnaround churches." I saw how these difficult changes caused anguish to women and men in ministry, and especially to women like me, married to men in ministry. I also witnessed what happened to women, men, and families when congregations refused to change but, instead, slipped further into purposelessness, dysfunction, and despair. My experiences brought me to see a strategic need for a practical, hope-filled book that could inspire kingdom servants to persevere until the painful pressures of change find relief.

I am a businesswoman married to a man who is an Executive Minister over a region of two hundred congregations. As his spouse, I have no title, no job description, and as far as I can tell, no official expectations. Official or not, however, I do have a position in the body of Christ. I have a role with expectations. Despite some of my best efforts, I am often seen as a reflection of my husband's position—a nonentity. This status, or non-status, depending on your viewpoint, is nonetheless important for the health of the congregations.

You might think that such an often ambiguous position would lead to frustration and, yes, even anger. And you might be surprised to know that you are right. Women Married to Men in Ministry are human after all, just like everyone else in the church. Despite challenges, however, there are also blessings. My relationship as a Woman Married to an Executive Minister puts me in contact with many other Women who are Married to

Men in Ministry. It also puts me in contact with gracious women serving in other ministry roles.

When I first became a part of "turnaround churches," I called us "The Women of Unpaved Roads." We were embarking on radical change in the church, and there were few role models for this particular journey. Often we faced situations where we had to, in essence, become our own role models. Sometimes we journeyed through places of incredible opportunity with deeply fulfilling challenges and blessings. Sometimes we found ourselves in discouraging, lonely places where only the naive would ever venture. I have since realized there were no roads at all—we had only contrails in the sky to follow.

A contrail is a vapor trail made from the exhaust of an airplane. You often see it in the sky after a plane passes over. Contrails are made of tiny ice crystals in the moist upper atmosphere. They can provide direction and comfort that you are not by yourself. As I shifted the metaphors of my journey from land to sky, I came to see myself as a copilot with my husband. I am not alone. Other women in ministry find themselves copiloting alongside men in ministry.

Have you ever been in a place with no roads? In the United States, we tend to take them for granted. Role models and teachers are much the same. They are part of everyday living. Living where there are none, means you are a pioneer. You have to hack through wilderness, mark the trail, and later, with help from others, build the roads. Without a role model, you have to hack through expectations and unknown relational terrain, but you also mark the successes and failures to guide others who are following you.

Some of the goals of our shared ministry are to help churches break new ground, transform lives, and bring people to the saving grace of our Lord. These are really all part of the greater vision to help churches live out the Great Commission. For many people this means extreme or radical change, finding ways to break the sound barrier. Yet leaders are often held back by particular ministry paradigms. There are "unsound" barriers they have to break too. One of the unsound barriers is the expectation of a "Pastor as Shepherd" and a Shepherd's wife versus a pilot pastor leader and a copilot or first officer.

But having to break the unsound barriers of a faulty ministry paradigm is not a task I realized *I* would need to do just because I married a man who is a minister. Together over the years, *as a couple*, we have learned to demolish the unsound barriers before we can break through the sound barrier in order to work effectively in new ministry approaches. Breaking through barriers, even hiking great chasms in our ministry, has led me to deeper places in my relationship with God than I thought I would ever be able to go. God continues to astound and amaze me with new flight plans, better equipment, fabulous crews, and even fresh vision.

Through this book, I believe God has given me the opportunity to validate our experiences as women in transformative ministries. I hope it will equip and inspire you. I hope that some of the trails I and other women like me have marked will provide you with guidance.

If you are married to a man in the ministry, please know that as you sit in the cockpit with your husband, you have earned your wings—often the angelic kind.

Growing Healthy Churches Takes Off

The context of my story of copiloting within transformational ministry started in 1997 with the American Baptist Churches of the West (ABCW), now known as Growing Healthy Churches. ABCW is one of thirty-four regions in the American Baptist Churches USA. The region then had 229 congregations located in northern California and northwest Nevada. Only thirty-seven of those churches—a mere 16 percent— were growing numerically. The rest were plateaued or declining. There were fewer than eight hundred baptisms in a year. A typical congregation comprised just one hundred people in attendance at worship services. Both pastors and congregations were aging; morale was low; and there was little hope for the future.

Just four years later in 2001, 72 percent of the congregations were experiencing numerical growth. The average attendance was 188, and there were more than eleven hundred more people collectively in attendance on Sundays than our congregations had in 1997. There were more than six thousand baptisms between 1999 and 2001! Obviously, something happened. What made the difference? I'll talk about how Growing Healthy Churches hit the bull's-eye of transformation in a later chapter. But for now, I'd like to focus on some of the more hidden sides of those changes.

When Growing Healthy Churches first embarked on the turnaround changes in 72 percent of our churches, we really didn't have a clue about the nonmonetary costs. We didn't know what it would extract from our women, men, and families. We didn't know how long it would take—and in many cases it was three years, others five years, and for some seven years. There really isn't a shortcut through this process; it takes time, desire, belief, vision, planning, risk-taking, perseverance, and courage. We have since discovered people can do almost anything if they can see an end to the pressure and can make sense of it. However, we didn't have that knowledge then.

But What Did Women and Families in Ministry Take On?

I was quite taken aback when I observed the expectations of women who were spouses of pastors or ordained ministers in their own right. As I began to interact with, listen to, and pray with many of these Women Married to Men in Ministry, I began to realize that there is a paradigm that many women accept and are expected to live in—the "shepherd's wife" stereotype. They're often called and known by the stereotype "pastors' wives." Unindoctrinated to this way of seeing women, I found this designation intriguing and demeaning. Have you heard such a term applied to attorneys' wives, doctors' wives, policemen's wives? In fact, most of us don't know if our attorneys have wives or where they live or how they raise their children. That, however, is not the case with the wife of a minister. There are systems of rules—mostly unwritten and unspoken—to which church people expect pastors' wives to conform. When the ordained minister is a female, most often her spouse is not called, "my pastor's husband."

Until Paul and I married fifteen years ago, I had no previous frame of reference regarding Women Married to Men in Ministry. When I looked at my ministry through the lens of being a copilot, the title "pastor's wife" didn't really fit. I discovered it represented an insidious system that hinders transformational ministry in the kingdom, not just of the Women Married to Men in Ministry specifically, but of the entire congregation. It undeservedly identifies a Woman Married to a Man in Ministry through someone else, through the position of her husband. It does not allow her to be seen as a unique woman of God in her own right.

I began to read many books directed to "pastors' wives." While many Women Married to Men in Ministry may have some common experiences, sometimes the only thing they have in common is being married to men in ministry. These books mainly gave advice about how to just survive while living in the glass house of ministry.

When I married a man who is a minister, I didn't realize I would be expected to take the path of the "pastor's wife" and fit a stereotype that was so grossly irrelevant to who I am and how my husband, Paul, and I view our relationship. This issue of being a "pastor's wife" struck a nerve in me, my collaborator, Barbara, and the other women who were interested in the writing of this book. We said, "We don't go to pastors' wives meetings because we're not like them." Really? Is this true?

But who are the women squeezed into that mold? What are they like? What do they want? Are my friends and I atypical or do other women feel similarly? These are the kinds of questions that we will address through the voices of women on this journey, as drawn from our own experiences, personal interviews, and extensive research.

My main message is this: **If we want to be successful in an era of dramatic global cultural changes, we must grow both healthy churches and healthy family relationships.** Healthy ministers, both men and women, must model the way. This dual goal of healthy churches and healthy families is impossible within the confines of the traditional stereotype of women as "pastors' wives." One reason this, perhaps seemingly innocent, designation cultivates unhealthy relationships is because it is confining and constricting. It also keeps what God may want to do through us in a box. It hinders the work of God in individuals and in the church. So, *Women Married to Men in Ministry* is about persevering through, soaring above, and giving voice to what holds women back from more effective ministry and a fulfilling life.

Let's Lift Off Together!

God has given me the opportunity to share some vital lessons and perspectives on women helping grow healthier churches. I trust these will ignite, illuminate, and empower you to shatter through the stained-glass ceilings of stereotypes and stir you as you find yourself in ministries of transformation.

I write not as a feminist theologian, but as a kingdom advocate and entrepreneurial activist—a God-created Fe-male.[1] I oppose church-culture constructs that hijack the Great Commission and suspend leaders in a web of meeting the consumerist demands of others. These demands invalidate my ministry, my person, and my relationships; and they also diminish the ministry, person, and relationships of my pastor husband. These demands put intolerable strain on our spiritual commitments, and they drive needless wedges between church leaders. Free of unnecessary bonds, we become empowered to pursue the kingdom stewardship requirements expected of all disciples.

In this book I use aeronautics metaphors to confront the personal challenges and systemic problems we must all address. I include insights from biblical role models with theological perspectives and share contemporary stories from pioneers of transformational ministries. (The stories we share are from real people. Unless otherwise noted in their accounts, personal names and details that identify the ministry have been removed.) Barbara and I trust this all works together as a biblically sound, practical, and hope-filled approach to change.

So, let's begin exploring new horizons and achieving new spiritual heights within Christ's kingdom!

PART ONE

Making It through the Shaking

BREAKING THE SOUND BARRIER: CHANGING TIMES, CHANGING PARADIGMS

Regarding the challenge of change, Machiavelli wrote in 1513, "There is nothing more difficult to plan, more doubtful of success, nor more dangerous to manage than the creation of a new system. For the initiator has the enmity of all who would profit by the preservation of the old institutions and merely lukewarm defenders of those who would gain by the new ones" (*The Prince*). This is certainly true worldwide.

William Bridges, in his book *Managing Transitions*, distinguishes organizational change from personal transitions as our response to change.[1] Change is easy—it happens naturally. It's the transition that is difficult—it has to happen intentionally. The story of Growing Healthy Churches represents a number of intentional strategies that reflect new ways of thinking and acting. You can read a full description of the vision, mission, strategies, and tactics in *Hit the Bullseye* (Nashville: Abingdon Press, 2003) by Paul Borden. As a result of the successful change and transformation of churches in our region, Growing Healthy Churches has become a national, and international, multidenominational movement in the church. Here is a very condensed version of our first conference. Then I'll share how it relates to the problem of faulty perspectives and approaches that hinder authentic ministries of transformation.

Our National and Global Journey

The first "Hit the Bull's Eye Conference" was held in June 2006. People attended from thirty denominations, twenty states, and three countries besides the United States—Canada, Australia, and New Zealand. The Bull's Eye Conference featured twenty-four pastor leaders who led the transitions within our own geographical region of northern California and northwest Nevada. There were ten panel discussion groups, two of which were made up of Women Married to Men in Ministry and another of couples in ministry.

Without a doubt, the changes that have occurred within our region have been nothing short of miraculous and are following God's Great Commission to go and make disciples. These changes have required incredible focus, time, hard work, and sacrifice, and they challenged what someone has called "the seven last words of the church": *we've never done it that way before.*

Still, we found there is a tremendous desire for renewal, change, and transformation of churches and denominations using the Bull's Eye principles. But this system requires people to think and act differently in order for deep changes to take place. The seven first words of the new paradigm are: *we can't do it that way again.* There *is* another way.

This is especially true regarding Women Married to Men in Ministry and the stereotypical image of them as "pastors' wives." Our conference in 2006 explored the unique position of Women Married to Men in Ministry, their view of the system of expectations, and their responses to it. This was the first time we'd ever heard of such a panel discussion being offered, and postconference evaluations stated that this was one of the most valuable parts of the event.

What Can a Turnaround Paradigm Look Like? Two Contemporary Examples

Our typical question about turnaround churches involves "What?" A much better question would involve "Who?" Who could a turnaround church look like? The following turnaround snapshots reflect the personal experiences of two ministerial couples who benefited from using our Bull's Eye principles and partnering with our consultants.

Sam and Doris had been called into ministry together and served a number of congregations as co-pastors. All of these congregations had been small and ineffective in reaching out to their communities. Their current congregation, a fifteen-year-old church plant, never had more than 120 people in worship. It was dominated by one lay couple who wanted everyone involved in their large Bible study ministry; yet all the study of the Bible had not produced much, if any, growth through conversions. We say we believe the Scriptures are the living word of God. How could they have so little impact if they were being communicated accurately and vividly? What was missing? Why was this Bible study a stagnant pool rather than life-giving water for the soul?

During a weekend consultation session, the Bull's Eye consultant confronted the lay leaders who admitted that when the church started, they and others were much more open to sharing the gospel with strangers than they were now. The consultant also encouraged Sam and Doris to become leader pastors in this church and equip people for Great Commission ministry, not act as if they were in a "hospital church" where the only way they could serve would be as chaplain caregivers.

The results of their initial work to shift paradigms have been nothing short of miraculous. In a very short time, the congregation has seen new growth and excitement. People are contributing their dollars, time, and energy for outreach. The congregational coach is helping both Sam and Doris learn how to behave consistently as leaders, with their major task being to keep the congregation on target in fulfilling its mission and vision.

Stewart has been leading a turnaround congregation that has seen major changes in six years. When Stewart and his wife, Leah, arrived, there were forty in worship. People from another turnaround congregation in their denomination, not liking what happened at their previous church, attended Stewart's congregation to make sure that his congregation would not adopt an attitude of change. During those six years of ministry, Stewart—with support from his denomination—not only helped those resistant people exit, he led the congregation to an average worship attendance of 250 while reaching out to the surrounding community.

When asked about his biggest learning experience, Stewart says,

> My wife, Leah, and I had to understand that God called us to lead. We also learned that in the midst of great strife, all we had was God. If we were going to serve our God well, we needed to stay, be firm, and be willing to

risk all. The result has been a miracle. God has intervened, and the congregational controllers are all gone. We are no longer hostages! We are seeing our community being reached through ministries of evangelism, compassion, and mercy.

Those anecdotes barely introduce Sam and Doris and Stewart and Leah. We'll share more from the stories of other leaders in turnaround churches in other chapters. Meanwhile, let's look at some of the dynamics that maintain old paradigms and create barriers to transformation in this new world.

Dynamics of Staying Static: Misusing the Power of Metaphors and Stereotypes

All paradigms use metaphors and stereotypes. Metaphors compare a significant number of particulars and processes between two different things—almost viewing them as twins. Thus, they create memorable ways for us to reflect on our world. Scripture is full of rich metaphors. For instance, Jesus is the lamb of God, bread of life, living water.

Metaphors serve as powerful methods of communication. Metaphors help empower, give voice, vision, and understanding. They can assist us in our mental images of ourselves, and they can cultivate an atmosphere for metamorphosis, change marked by an alteration of character and/or appearance. However, if a metaphor is insufficient, misunderstood, or interpreted out of context, it can stifle growth and change at both the personal and corporate levels. For instance, if we view our church as a "hospital for the spiritually wounded," it is too easy to focus on care without cure for those who have been traumatized by life's experiences and never help these individuals move toward wholistic health. It's just hard for people who see themselves only as sick to see themselves well; they have too much investment in reaping the benefits of their wounds.

Stereotypes serve as a quick method to label a person according to collective characteristics (that is, a group to which they belong) rather than their unique, individual characteristics. The original use of the word *stereotype* came from the field of printing. It described making multiple stampings from a single mold.

Words have power, and history repeatedly shows that labeling individuals or groups by stereotyping has many long-term ramifications. For instance, some stereotypes create scapegoats that can lead to segregation, discrimination, and conflict. Think of what you may have heard about how the British view the French, how the French view the Americans, or how Evangelicals, mainline Protestants, Pentecostals, Fundamentalists, Catholics, Charismatics, and Orthodox all tend to view one another.

Current church-culture metaphors and stereotypes support a static paradigm, not a dynamic movement of growth for God's kingdom. So, I believe that when we operate within the present interpretation typical of church culture, we do a great deal of damage to both ministry couples and the growth of the church, the body of Christ. I'd like us to get more specific and look at two key metaphors and related stereotypes that create barriers to copilot and transformational ministry. First, we'll explore the metaphor of Pastor as Shepherd versus the Pastor as Shepherd-Leader. Later, we'll look at its counterpart for the wife of a minister.

Battle of Two Metaphors: "Pastor as Shepherd" versus "Pastor as Shepherd-Leader"

I agree with Paul Borden's definition of the pastor metaphor with the shepherd being an entrepreneur—the shepherd made his living from raising sheep—as described in *Hit the Bullseye* (pp. 20–23). I would say that more than the misinterpretation of words, however, about who a shepherd is and what a shepherd does, is the picture of a shepherd we see in our mind's eye from childhood. The image may have no relationship at all to the Scripture. But, like it or not, our imaginations are shaped and our thoughts are formed by the pictures we see.

The picture I am thinking of typically portrays Jesus standing in a rural scene with his clothing perfectly draped and sparkling clean. His face is placid, calm, kind, and gentle. He has a flock of soft woolly sheep gathered around his feet. Off in the distance, other sheep are grazing calmly, surrounded by green pastures and flowing streams. Also notice that most of these pictures feature a light-complexioned man with European features, light eyes, and blond or brown hair that is long and flowing enough to be used in advertisements for shampoo and conditioner!

The image does not embody a person of Jewish heritage, as we know Jesus to be. It also gives a misleading representation of what it meant to be a shepherd. Yet, for many, this picture persists in their mind's eye as some romantic notion that life in Christ is a field day with no wolves, enough food, nice weather, no worries—an easy life. In reality, during biblical times, shepherds were considered unsavory characters. There were hot, sweaty days, with long, sleepless nights. It was a poor man's profession, with the unenviable task of trying to keep obstinate, easily spooked sheep out of harm's way.

A more realistic metaphor of the shepherd has been understood throughout the ages in agricultural societies. But in today's industrialized and technological culture of city dwellers, there are people in the United States and around the world who have never seen a sheep and don't know what a shepherd does. Nevertheless, this flawed image of placid rural life is still used throughout churches. So, if we look at the real role of a shepherd, we need to leave the comforts of our childhood picture behind and see that shepherds were businesspeople. Their livelihood came from raising sheep for milk, food, and clothing for their families and to sell or barter with others. They also mated sheep to guarantee future business resources.

We take comfort in hearing about the shepherd going after the one lost sheep that went astray. The truth is, the shepherd would go after a lost sheep two times, and then he would break its leg, take it back to camp, splint it, and keep it close to himself. This was a difficult lesson so obstinate sheep would learn to hear the shepherd, listen to his voice, and follow.

The Scripture is very clear that it is the obligation of sheep to listen and to follow. That means a shepherd is a leader who is supposed to be followed. The biblical norm is a "Shepherd-Leader Pastor" model. The two-pronged problem is that many pastors do not see themselves as the leader, and congregations often view pastors as caretakers who must run around day and night, tending to all the sheep. In this insufficient model, the pastor follows the sheep.

Where did this faulty metaphor of the placid pastor as shepherd develop? I have concluded that it is certainly more culturally picturesque than scriptural. And so is its counterpart, the "Shepherd's Wife."

The "Shepherd's Wife" Metaphor

The shepherd's-wife metaphor comes with a long list of usually unspoken and unwritten expectations for Women Married to Men in Ministry.

This list ranges from playing a musical instrument, heading committees, providing childcare, and attending every function the church offers to anything else that supposedly needs to be done. (As some congregants unfortunately jest, "We got two for the price of one!") Many times she is unfairly scrutinized about her appearance, her housekeeping skills, and her philosophy of parenting. Those are just a few of the expectations.

As finite persons, we all have unresolved issues, either from childhood or trauma or just from living in a world with hurtful people. When, however, a person constantly tries to fit into an ill-fitting mold or a pattern of exaggerated expectations, whether from herself or others, she will burn out, drop out, or serve under duress. Either way, a very unhealthy pattern emerges. If the pattern persists, happiness and abundant living drain out of her like blood from her veins, leaving behind drudgery and dread, fear and unhappiness, depression, and, eventually, spiritual death. Who would choose to live like that? There is a better way, which leads to a question.

Why in the twenty-first century are we operating under such a burdensome paradigm in the first place? I can find no biblical mandate for this shepherd's-wife cultural stereotype, which is where I think these false expectations come from. My understanding of Scripture is that we are all called once we have accepted Christ as our personal Savior. Some then are gifted as teachers and leaders with skills that can be used in the church. Perhaps the second part of this equation comes from whether a woman embraces her husband's position as an unassailable calling or simply sees his gifts being used in a position of employment in God's service.

I think until we look at this faulty perspective and begin to define who we are as women and what roles we will take in the area of ministry, it is like putting a new patch on an old garment, wearing it day in and day out until the fabric begins to tear and separate. It just isn't working. And it definitely won't work where radical change is taking place within the church.

Misunderstanding of the Shepherd Pastor metaphor is particularly damaging for a woman ordained in ministry who is in a pastoral position. It reinforces the caregiver model, leaving no room for the leadership model. Rather, it relegates her to a supporting role with the idea of inherent feminine caregiving—that she is just too subservient and too ineffective to lead and take charge. It leaves her with mundane tasks and busywork with little or no authority to lead. The female minister is expected to attend endless meetings and do regular visitation taking her off course and task for leadership. Oftentimes when a female minister does try to lead she is referred to pejoratively as a female dog. Congregations need to be taught that collaboration, teamwork, and integration are powerful leadership skills. *More on this later.*

First and foremost, we are women created by God as individuals, and this unchangeable, *universal reality* must be honored above all else regarding varying *local cultural perspectives and expectations.* We are daughters, granddaughters, sisters, nieces. Some of us become wives and mothers. We are each given special gifts. Some women will want to use those gifts and talents in a career outside the home, while others may see their careers and services develop within the church or the home.

Operating under the traditionally accepted metaphors of Shepherd and Shepherd's wife becomes even more difficult and the expectations even more demanding when changes are introduced into congregations. Often, congregants who have become accustomed to control shift from passive control to out-of-control behavior—as change is initiated, some of the congregation will lose the role that provided significance, and as a result they often attack the pastor leader and the woman married to him.

That is the context in which this book is written: to help women as copilots in mission define who we are and how we will serve in the twenty-first century. The contributions of women have to be recognized historically and globally. Women can no longer be a footnote. We have many wonderful examples of women from Scripture who show us possibilities, especially during times of trial and transformation.

There are also many courageous contemporary women and men who are leading the way through systemic change to growing healthy churches— the unsung heroes of the Great Commission Transformation's work. Their stories, like the one that follows, will appear throughout the book.

Giving Voice 1
A Midwest "Church Widow" Experiences Hope

I had grown very frustrated with the unrealistic expectations that the church was placing on my husband. He was the pastor of the church, and it seemed they expected him to do all of the ministry.

He was expected to visit all the sick, including those physically ill in hospitals as well as those who were upset and unhealthy because they were not getting enough of the pastor's time "holding their hand" and handing out "spiritual pacifiers." He was to also

---

visit and care for the "shut-ins" and those in nursing homes and assisted living. He was expected to counsel families with problems and spend time inspiring and leading the youth and children of the church. He was to oversee and provide direction to a day-care ministry as well as write an inspiring article for the monthly newsletter.

Along with those responsibilities, he was to prepare two sermons and a weekly Bible study for the consumption of those who saw their primary purpose in the church to be the continual evaluator of the pastor. They would evaluate and criticize as to how well they felt he was doing in comparison to what they liked in previous pastors.

And if he had any remaining time, he was expected to reach out into the community and bring hurting and unchurched people into relationship with God.

I painfully watched as my husband worked long days attempting to get all the things done that the church leaders expected of him. He worked hard in order to hopefully be able to free up a day or so that he could devote to reaching out into the community for the cause of Christ. As a result, he didn't take a day off. He felt he needed that "day off" to do outreach into the community as somehow that was his day and thus did not cheat the church.

I was the one who got cheated. My husband was out most evenings either in meetings, Bible study, or visiting with people. He was just not available for his family. I was angry at the church for making me feel like a widow, raising three kids. I went into a dark place for a while. I suffered alone, feeling that I was being selfish if I expected my husband to neglect the lost and hurting people of our community who desperately needed to know God.

But I was becoming desperate in my own way as I sought to make sense of what God had called us to do. It was our first church to pastor after graduation from seminary. There was so much we did not know about pastoring and leading a church. But I knew something wasn't right about this picture. In my darkness, a light began to flicker as God spoke to my husband through his nine-year-old daughter. On this particular evening, he was headed out the door once again when she asked him, "Daddy, when can I get one of those appointments with you?" As he looked over at me, I could tell he was broken as he finally was able to hear what I had been saying for some time—it was time for a change.

From our Midwestern perspective, something very interesting was happening in the region of churches known then as American Baptist Churches of the West (now Growing Healthy Churches). We had heard about a vision for doing church differently. We were told about how churches were restructuring themselves in order to allow the pastor to truly lead the church toward being outward focused. Every member was to serve as a minister and the pastor was not expected to do all the work! *We're interested! Where do we sign up?*

We moved to a church of a little over one hundred. They had just gone through a time of assessment with the region and had voted to place their constitution in abeyance for a period of three years in order to allow the church to move in this new direction. Robert Quinn, in his book *Deep Change*, uses the phrase "walking naked into the land of uncertainty."[2] That is what it felt like for us as we left behind all the things we knew and loved in the Midwest and moved halfway across the country.

Quinn talks about the difference between "incremental change" and "deep change," stating that incremental change usually does not disrupt our past patterns but rather is an extension of the past. Also, in incremental change, one feels they are in control. Deep change, says Quinn, requires new ways of thinking and behaving. It is change that is major in scope, discontinuous with the past, and generally irreversible. Deep change means surrendering control.

We were definitely going through deep change, and it would be necessary if we were going to be able to effectively lead this congregation through the deep change that they needed. The church had also made a decision to "walk naked into the land of uncertainty." As God would have it, we would learn to walk this journey of deep change and transformation together. It has been both a painful and positive experience.

The painful part primarily involved the grieving and letting go of the things from the past; for both my family personally as well as the church as a whole. For us as a family, we had made a big commitment and had taken a pretty big step and thus it was not easy to go back. For the church, there would be a continual temptation to go back and not follow through with what had been put in motion.

My husband received hurtful, attacking letters as people worked through the deep change and the pain of letting go of the past in order to embrace the new reality God had for us. We learned that it was one thing for people to *say* they were committed to this change but another to actually *be* committed to the process. We experienced the pain of passive-aggressive people, as well as "aggressive, aggressive" people!

But through it all, God has been faithful to his promise. God has gone before us, and we have learned what it means to wait upon the Lord as God moves some people out the way and humbles others and changes hearts. Certainly, we have been humbled before God, and our hearts have been changed in this transformation process.

How we are experiencing church today is so much healthier to the pastor, his family, and the church. As with giving birth to a child, the painful aspects are lost within the positive experience that we have today. The church has grown to over four hundred. Members are expected to be ministers. My husband focuses significant amounts of his time on reaching our community for Christ and making disciples for Jesus Christ as members learn how to minister, visit, and care for one another. My husband is home most evenings. His wife and kids are much happier and healthier and, as a result, so is he.

Biblical Women of Strength and Character

Speaking of expectations and making changes, I find dozens of biblical women who show strength of character by taking risks. They show passion, courage, flexibility, a God-oriented mind-set, wisdom, positive outlook, and responsibility. They break through the cultural expectations of their own eras to accomplish extraordinary things.

The woman of Proverbs 31 is very entrepreneurial. She is active in both private and public spheres. Women's ability in the marketplace and in real estate is no less esteemed today. We see her being talked about as wisdom itself.

We have many wonderful examples of women in Scripture who served without being servile, who showed care without merely being a caregiver, who persevered without being passive. They did not wait for institutional authorization or permission. Instead, they moved based on the authority and power of their position as a chosen daughter of God. These stories of role-model women of the Word come down to us from as much as four millennia before our time. And yet, their relevance for today gives us new perspectives.

Some of the women who have gone before us have exhibited a boldness and self-determination that carved out a space of their own, in spite of patriarchal constraints. They include: Tamar, Rahab, Hannah, Miriam, Huldah, Abigail, Puah, Shiphrah, Ruth, Deborah, and Esther from the Old Testament; and Mary the mother of Jesus, Mary and Martha, Mary Magdalene, Dorcas, Priscilla, Eunice, and Lydia from the New Testament.

The most courageous women challenged some kind of oppression. We have stories of women who dared. We see a woman leading troops into battle—an example of both political and spiritual leadership, a woman hiding spies in her home, and another asserting her right to bear a child. We see women taking decisive action at great personal risk. There is the woman who providentially became a queen but chose to become an advocate for her people, thus saving their lives—women in business, midwives, and prophets. A woman poured essential oil on Jesus as an offering of her love and devotion; this one woman understood what the disciples could not grasp—Jesus would die. A woman took ointment and fragrant spices to an empty tomb. Women were forgiven of sins; healed in body, mind, and spirit; and taught spiritual truths. Women were commissioned to spread the gospel of Christ.

But, Jesus entered into a society in which the custom was for men to thank God daily that they had not been born a woman, a slave, or a foreigner.[3] By his words and by his example, Jesus broke the sound barrier and challenged this cultural practice that denigrated women. Instead, he welcomed women, talked with them, and taught them. He broke the silence and bridged the gap.

Women played a vital role in the earthly life of Christ, from his mother, Mary, to women followers who gave financial means from their hearts in order to follow the teachings of Jesus and support him and his disciples. Women in the first-century church opened their hearts and homes so that the first believers in Christ had a place to gather for worship, communion, and study. Jesus' tenderness toward women is displayed in his actions toward the woman with the issue of blood, toward the woman at the well, and toward the woman who first carried the message of the resurrection. His behavior toward women followers confirmed the authenticity of his words that "whoever does the will of my Father in heaven is my brother and sister and mother" (Matthew 12:50). These women are not anonymous—the Scriptures etch their names and their stories in history forever. As Women in Ministry, we, too, are *not* anonymous to God, and our work also forever changes the course of history.

This is our inheritance as women who are disciples of Jesus—these are some of our "sheroes."

Missing the Bull's-Eye

As Growing Healthy Churches expands into a worldwide movement, it is my prayer and hope that people will be able to learn from what we did well and also from areas where we didn't. As I observe the change process now from farther along in the journey, I can see several areas where I believe we missed the bull's-eye referred to in Paul Borden's book. *We have not been very intentional in promoting or protecting the health and well-being of transformational couples or of ministerial families.*

While we put great emphasis on growing healthy churches, we needed (and still need) to put equal emphasis on growing healthy relationships in ministry couples and their families. In later chapters, I will share our understanding of where we missed the bull's-eye and also some ways to strengthen your ministry relationships, keeping them healthy, vibrant, and on target. So, I trust that those who follow us will have greater success than we did in both family and church health, with less collateral damage. This will be critical to sustaining a movement of transformational congregations whose people fulfill the Great Commission. If we do not hit the bull's-eye of healthy ministers, ministry couples, and families, we cannot fly as we should, with both wings and with all systems "Go!"

Milestones to Mach 1

The Wright brothers' flight lasted twelve seconds and covered 120 feet. The power of the X-41A aircraft lets it travel fifteen miles in eleven seconds. Now that's progress! But there were many years and many stalls in between. A hinge point in aeronautics came with a literal breakthrough.

Some time ago, I read about Chuck Yeager, the aeronautics pioneer who broke the sound barrier in 1947. Chuck's story told about the violent shaking of the aircraft just as he came up to the point of breaking the sound barrier. This point was invisible, but nevertheless very real. The violent shaking always caused him to back off the throttle and abandon the mission. Until one day he wondered what would happen if he were to push through the violent shaking. So, he pushed the throttle forward and hung on, nearly being knocked unconscious. The very second he was through the sound barrier, the air was as smooth as silk. He observed, "Grandma could be sitting up there sipping lemonade, it was so still."[4]

So, with that as our metaphor, we asked ministry couples in our transitioning churches if they would push through the violent shaking and quaking of the change process. Much to their credit, most of the couples stepped up to the challenge. This was not an easy task. It was downright scary and painful most of the time, as we did not know how long the gap would be between the violent shaking and the smooth sailing.

What Chuck Yeager described was Mach 1; he was going 660 miles per hour the first time he broke the sound barrier. Now we can go hypersonic speeds of Mach 8 or even Mach 10—6,800 miles per hour—with no sense of violent shaking of the aircraft anymore. Because Chuck was willing and courageous enough to find out how to break the sound barrier, we now build planes designed with a narrower, sleeker nose and swept-back wings. These allow planes to slip through the sound barrier without a blip, equipped for the twenty-first century.

Since the time I read that book about Chuck Yeager, I have discovered that a few short years after he broke the sound barrier, two women also broke the sound barrier: Jacqueline Cochran (1905?–1980) from the United States and Diana Barnato Walker (born 1918) from Great Britain. That opened the way for women into space exploration, with Sally Ride being the first female astronaut on a flight mission. These pioneers were not unlike the women who anointed Jesus with expensive fragrant oil before the crucifixion, or the woman at the well who was perhaps the first evangelist, or, in more recent times, the nationally and internationally known Bible teachers, healers, evangelists, and authors like Aimee Semple McPherson, Kathryn Kuhlman, Joyce Meyer and Anne Graham Lotz opening the way for women to proclaim the good news through evangelism.

Learning to lead the church through change is like training to become an astronaut for a trip into outer space. The preliminaries and the experiences will take us into worlds never traveled before. We'll definitely be out of our comfort zone! Flying through the sound barrier and beyond is a great metaphor for church transformation.

We designed this book to be your in-flight handbook. Just as a preview: A safe flight and successful turnaround begin with sound judgment and good preparation. The pilot and copilot carefully plan and perform a pre-flight check prior to departure. Before passengers enter the aircraft, the airline mechanic checks the electronic and mechanical instruments and reviews the trajectory of the flight. Likewise, a pastor will need to employ similar techniques. It is the pastor's responsibility to plan a flight that is safe for all on board, including the copilot. Keeping God's Great Commission is the focal point. Growing healthy churches and growing healthy families is the desired destination.

The liftoff can be described as heading into the wind. This action will require plenty of oxygen—the breath of the Holy Spirit—for a successful launch, with flight attendant instructions to put your own mask on first before helping others if something goes amiss. Plenty of the fuel of faith will be needed to complete the voyage. No one wants to be unable to finish the mission. And, as important as liftoff is, landing is equally crucial—to descend, touch down, and return to mission control for debriefing and a new assignment. Mission complete!

New Paradigm Leaders

The world has changed and twenty-first-century, Mach-10 ministry requires new paradigm leaders. These women and men exhibit courage under fire and have the strength to withstand powerful opposition. These new kinds of leaders offer, by example, lessons that are universal; all people can learn from those who helped them minister effectively.

Unlike a traditional compass pointing to magnetic North, which can fluctuate, a gyrocompass interacts with the force produced by the earth's rotation. When set to the magnetic compass, the gyrocompass will maintain a north-south orientation of the gyroscopic spin axis, thereby providing a stable directional reference. No matter how unstable the environment, it always points to true North.

One of the most important things anyone can do is to establish true North, which we know to be Christ. This will build a level of confidence from the inside out and also an assurance for the people around us. It will give us a tether of stability so that we can experiment, take risks, and make necessary repairs.

New paradigm leaders are constantly reinventing themselves to accommodate a wider focus. If they lose contact with their true North, they stop. Or, if they realign, they foster God-given creativity and nurture new ideas. Many of the women whom I have been privileged to meet through these last years are truly pioneers with great courage. Some might not even recognize themselves as leaders . . . yet. But they are. As this book progresses, we'll share many of their stories as transformational leaders and detail the perspectives and skills needed for smooth flying through the sound barrier and beyond toward Mach-10 ministry.

CHAPTER TWO

REALITIES OF LIVING IN SYSTEMIC CHANGE

Fit to Serve

Ministry service always creates a crucible for personal growth. Bryan Cutshall offers some sobering statistics on this reality in his book *Where Are the Armorbearers?*

He describes how difficult the environment is for pastors. Almost a third of all pastors leave their congregations due to conflict even though such conflict is usually caused by less than eight people. Twenty-five percent of pastors relocate every year while the average associate stays less than twenty-four months. For many years now, more congregations in the United States have been dying than have been started. More than one thousand pastors a year are terminated without cause, with many of those congregations repeating this act with following pastors. The divorce rate among clergy has risen 65 percent in the last two decades with two-thirds of clergy spouses saying that they are unhappy with their marriage and most pastors spending little time during the week with their families. Almost one-half of all seminary graduates leave the ministry after five years while more than two-thirds of all pastors say they have no one they consider as their personal friend.[1]

In the book of Genesis, God created Eve to complement Adam. In 1 Corinthians 11:1-16, the apostle Paul affirms that this relationship was designed to create mutual dependency (v. 11). The man needs the help of the woman God created, and the woman needs the help of the man whom she was designed to complete.

In Growing Healthy Churches, we have found that, at the beginning stages, ministry in the midst of systemic church change amplifies the level of conflict, loss, and pain. It is not easy, even on those we might consider the most mature of pastors. And it inevitably affects their spouses and families in adverse ways. Pastors and the women they are married to are meant to help each other, to depend on each other, and support each other. For this they must be fit, able, and willing.

In this chapter, I'd like us first to hear one woman's story of moving through systemic change and the impact it had on her. Then we will consider some core learnings and skills we need in order to address qualitatively healthy transformation for pastors, their spouses and families, congregations, judicatories, and denominations. All of these passengers have a role to play in whether growth turns out wholistic and healthy or partial and anemic.

Constructing a New Fuselage for Twenty-first-Century Ministry: Adapting the Ancient Wineskins Metaphor

Although the purpose and destination of the good news of Christ remain the same in all ages—namely, to transform the human heart—the wood-and-canvas biplane of the past century can't carry the message in the supersonic era of today.

Assuming we want to be obedient to the Great Commission, what do we need to do as women and men in leadership to be ready for sustainable ministry in changing times? We need both personal and corporate retrofits. Mach-10 ministry in the twenty-first century requires the right stuff of visionary leadership, flexible systems, and cooperative partnerships. Inflexible stereotypes and antiquated systems do not support paradigm change but rather sustain the status quo. So, just as supersonic planes are engineered to sustain the forces of breaking the sound barrier, future-oriented churches need systems, structures, and relationships to support new vintage ministry.

A helpful biblical metaphor when thinking about systemic change is that of the vessel for the wine, called a wineskin. Jesus said, "No one cuts up a fine silk scarf to patch old work clothes; you want fabrics that match. And you don't put your wine in cracked bottles" (Matthew 9:16-17 *The Message*). He communicated this timeless truth to people in his era through an illustration common to their agrarian culture. They lived and worked in vineyards, and understood the implications and risks of pouring precious new wine into dried and leaking wineskins. Just as the old vessel would burst from the pressure brought about by fermentation, old church structures will not withstand the pressures of change now.

In transforming church cultures, as with winemaking, the first stage of change comes with the crush—and leaders are the first batch of grapes. Turning grapes into the sweet liquid of juice for wine requires them to first be broken. Ministers and Women Married to Men in Ministry may also be broken open for the flavor of our lives and ministry to be released. As we move forward to help others, we may find ourselves humbled as we come to realize that what used to work for us no longer produces sweet results.

One Woman Married to a Man in Ministry in a transitioned church describes the crush in this way:

> My story begins with a calling by God in my life. Had I not felt that direct call with his divine direction in my life, I don't know if I would have had the courage, much less the desire, to stick it out through some very dark times. My husband had been a pastor for several years in a system that provided a lot of security. He had been feeling God calling him in a different direction—to leave what he knew to be a secure future and follow God fully wherever that may lead him, to be able to fully realize his passion for the lost. That desire to be obedient to God's call put to test what we really believed about doing whatever it takes to reach people for Christ, including the sacrifice of some very dear relationships.

Just as the progression from the biplane to the space shuttle, the wineskins metaphor encourages us to keep constructing new vessels—ones wisely crafted with the best possible match of materials, weights, speeds, and distances to optimize our congregational "aircraft" for the kind of journey we intend to accomplish.

Giving Voice 2
My Journey through Systemic Change

Fitting into the new structures after you've been used to the old ones for so long causes grief and loss.

I am the wife of a judicatory staff member. After twenty-five years of serving in local churches, my husband became part of a regional staff. His position and ministry seemed custom-made for him. Once he became familiar with it, he was effective, valued, appreciated, and fulfilled.

Nine years into this way of life, a new leader came and brought complete change. This change disbanded a lifetime system as we knew it. The previous system came to a screaming halt. Visionaries don't worry about the details, and the new system was to be "written as we went." My husband was a detail person and one of the very few kept on staff from the previous system. Additional leaders arrived with the new CEO. Suddenly my husband was treading water personally and professionally.

The denomination made a lot of training available to pastors and lay leaders in the entire region. Pastors who easily embrace change—about one-third of them—were rewarded, excited, and on their way. The remaining two-thirds of the pastors really struggled. Professionally, my husband and I were being bombarded by those who felt they were sold out—pastor and laity alike. We—my husband and I—lived with one foot in two camps: the previous and the new. We were committed to the new but were uncertain where it was going since the new system was "being written as we went." We prayed that God was leading the new leader and that the "new" was of the Lord. In fairness, the trainings were exceptional, useful, needful, thrilling. At the same time we grieved the losses—ours personally and professionally and the multiple disruptions of church after church not yet able to embrace systemic change. Other people frequently expressed their losses to us with tones of concern and emotions of anger. Fears of the unknown and the future were a shroud, especially to those who lived decades in the previous system. We were definitely in the middle, hearing the voices of the grief and trying to support the change.

I wearied of it all. Personally, I much prefer for a new solution to be in place before removing the old system, and this preference unnerved me. It felt like a big weight. Multiple conversations with people who were not yet able to embrace the change also became like boulders on my shoulders. News of this unease, this unrest and resistance, traveled many miles, and people we had known for years from other parts of the country were cool and distant from us when we saw them at our National Assembly, reflecting positions of friends they knew here in the region. That was painful.

The yet still heavier despairing part for us was that my husband became depressed and wasn't sure that he could leap the chasm. There didn't seem to be a place or space for him to contribute in the new system. This lasted some while and affected us greatly. I was deeply worried for him and for us. Where would this take us? Would the other shoe drop? Then what? I was dealing with huge amounts of uncertainty at many levels—fearful and angry at the cost to others, my husband, and me. I became sick of the whole scene and felt like I was drowning. I once talked with a friend not involved in our denomination, but no answers came. I fought daily for perspective. Some days I had it. Many days I did not. Life and ministry were upside down for eighteen months or more. Fear, grief, loss, anxiousness were familiar companions, which altered everything.

Meanwhile, training continued the next two years or so. Policy evolved more; additional pastors and laypeople embraced the change. With counseling, my husband was able to adjust. Appreciation for the training increased; excitement and anticipation rose. Not all pastors or laypeople were able to switch to the new system, but the majority did. The new system is fruitful, and God is blessing. Lives are being changed for Jesus' sake, both in existing congregations and in multiple new church starts with numerous new conversions, baptisms, and maturing Christians. Praise God!

Systemic change is a major shift, and it was traumatic. Preparation for change would have been helpful. Had we identified losses and brought people along, that still may have resulted in resistance from some. But the shock would have been less and the adjustment for change would have been easier.

Postscript: Writing the story of my journey through systemic change brought back some intense feelings and painful memories of people's responses, my own included. I realized again that the longer people had lived with one system in place, the harder it was to accept and implement the new. It flew in the face of loyalty, commitment, and what they/I held dear. Never mind that the system wasn't working. It felt like betrayal to leave it.

Ten Lessons from Leaders of Systemic Change

All parties affected by systemic change have important things to learn for it to work well—pastors, spouses and families, congregation members, judicatory staff. If I were asked to give an "executive summary" of the lessons we've gleaned in ten years of church transformation ministry, here is what I would report:

1. *Stop the Addiction to Consumption.* Congregations that have been on a plateau or in decline for more than three years are like a person with an addiction. In their case they were addicted to a social network and a church created to serve their consumerist needs. Intervention is required to catalyze change. Without intervention, healing, and sustained systemic change, these congregations will continue to be religious consumers who are disobedient to Christ's Great Commission for his church, which involves producing disciples.

2. *Multilevel Leadership Is Essential.* The "turnaround pastor" must be a leader, or at least have the ability to exercise leadership behaviors. However, most pastors cannot lead such systemic change alone. Pastors and their spouses need help from the outside. A key and fundamental role for denominational personnel is to **stand with** leaders/pastors, their spouses, and their families; **resource them** personally and professionally; and **risk the potential loss** of congregational dollars and affirmation. This involves recognizing the spouses' contributions as copilots as essential to the success of the ministry.

3. *Seek Valid Denominational Roles in Congregational Life.* The truth is, most people do not know or care what a church's denominational affiliation is. It's like the working mechanism of an airplane. We don't necessarily want to look at what's under the hood, we just want it to take us safely to our destination. There are only two valid reasons for denominations to exist—first, to help congregations transform and then to help them reproduce. Denominations play other key managerial and administrative roles. But if the Great Commission is not prominent in terms of how denominational resources are expended locally and globally, then that denomination has no right to exist. Maybe that is why so many denominations are approaching biblical irrelevance, and thus declining in membership.

4. Accountability Requires Discomfort. Pastors and denominational leaders who do not want to disrupt comfortable congregations must understand the realities: their passivity by *not* equipping people or holding them accountable amounts to abdication of their biblical responsibilities as Christian leaders. They fall woefully short as those who are required to serve God well. By their continued enabling of dysfunctional congregations, such pastors and leaders implicitly endorse the continual exercise of disobedient behaviors in the church. Thus, they themselves engage in carnal, "codependent" relationships that work against God's mission for his church. However, they are still accountable to the Great Shepherd-Leader for these antileadership practices, and congregation members are still accountable for their actions as well. When pastors finally *do* hold congregants accountable, that is often a key action that causes Women Married to Men in Ministry the most pain because accountability time is when many people begin leaving the church, resulting in broken relationships.

5. We Must Both Equip and Encourage Our Pastors, Spouses, and Ministerial Families. Many pastors are both unwilling and unprepared to lead systemic change. That is why they need equipping to know what to do and the encouragement of having someone stand with them as they do it. The bottom line is all about leadership and equipping those pastors who are willing to be or act like leaders and who will risk their jobs if necessary. (OK . . . take a deep breath!) Another part of that same bottom line is to resource and recognize their spouses and families as well. To achieve balanced "success" in systemic change, we must sustain a support system for both health and growth of the entire ministerial family unit, versus only church growth categorized by numerical increases. It is very helpful to receive training regarding change and transition. Women Married to Men in Ministry need an understanding of the issues involving the inevitability of conflict; this training can help provide objectivity that can assist them in depersonalizing what seem like personal attacks that can create a them-versus-us mind-set.

6. Preliminary Preparations Are Not the Same as Systemic Changes. Creating steps that lead to systemic change is very different from leading systemic change itself. The former gets a congregation ready for the ride ahead, and the latter takes them through the sound barrier and beyond. However, the more presystemic change that we can implement, the easier it will be to lead systemic change. (This is where the use of an intentional interim leader can be vital.) Pastors, particularly those who do not have outside help, may need to make small incremental preliminary changes for one to five years before leading systemic paradigm change. However, once systemic change is initiated, the pastor has only from one to two years to make it take root. It may then take another three to five years to make sure the congregation does not regress to old ways of behaving.

7. *Consider the Costs and Benefits for Leaders.* The costs of change and transition are more terrible than can be imagined until we break through and achieve systemic transformation. This initial change process will likely be a wilderness experience, with betrayal from unexpected people, lack of support from insiders and outsiders, and amplified pressures on leaders and their families. The violent shaking of personal, family, and corporate transformational processes usually knocks the spiritual wind right out of us. In an effort to catch your breath again, it is helpful to have a confidante with a listening ear and perhaps professional assistance through this violent shaking time. However, once we've broken through the sound barrier, then comes an important return on the investment. We finally get to do for the kingdom what motivated us to serve in ministry in the first place!

8. *Successful Transition Requires Dealing with the Losses of Change.* The core issues of resistance in congregations that fight change are actually issues of emotional grief attached to personal losses. People who previously found personal significance in holding positions in the church do not want to give them up. Their sense of significance involves control, power to influence the congregation, money, and "turf." Leaders must attempt to bring these people into the process with a compelling vision and personal ownership of a new place to serve. A thank-you often goes a long way in recognizing their past contributions. As James Belasco and Ralph Stayer aptly put it, change is hard because people "overestimate the value of what [they] currently have, and have to give up, and underestimate the value of what [they] may gain."[2] Although leaders should offer compassionate help and resources to those dealing with the losses of change, the leaders are not responsible for the choices made. Some resisters will become very supportive. Others will remain recalcitrant; the pain of their departing is necessary.

9. *Real Change Requires Long-term Changes in Behavior.* Anyone who has ever tried to change any habit—diet, smoking, drinking, and any number of things—knows how difficult it is to change and then sustain it. (For instance, in my business I had the opportunity to serve many medical professionals, and in conversation regarding change of habits most agree that 80 percent of people who undergo major surgery to repair heart attacks *do not significantly alter* the choices in diet and lack of exercise that can lead to the problems in the first place.) Systemic change in church is no different—the challenge is to get people to change behavior because when we refocus on the urgent mission of discipling people, we cannot have church as usual. However, congregations that say they want change usually mean something far different from what most pastors think. Often, the congregation's idea of change amounts to more people in church and more money in the budget—*as long as the culture of the congregation does not change and we can still be in control of how things are done*. To give way to "new wine and new mission," congregants must genuinely relinquish self-destructive control and adopt appropriate accountability. When they do, we have seen awesome kingdom results!

10. Renewal of Mission "Reinvigorates" Prior Investments. It is much more difficult to lead a congregation in a radical turnaround and systems transformation than to start a new church. However, the renewed investment is worth it when one sees facilities sitting on valuable properties being used once again to achieve grand missions that produce changed lives and communities for the kingdom of God. Just imagine it!

How God Shows Up in Our Transformation Process

The term *transformation* can mean so many different things that it can actually end up being empty of meaning. In *Women Married to Men in Ministry*, we focus on transformation as the larger process that involves *changes* and *transitions*.

William Bridges's book *Managing Transitions* helps us distinguish events that bring organizational changes and transition that comes from the personal processing of such changes. I have created the following illustrations, which reflect my understanding of Bridges's concepts. I believe this will help us understand the church transformation process, which includes both changes and transitions.

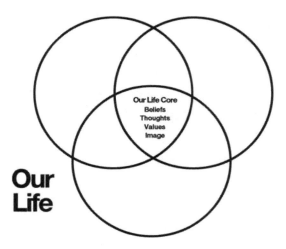

In this first illustration, I see the three circles representing the trinitarian nature of God, and the triune nature of our lives as those created in his image. The core area represents the intersection of our heart, soul, and mind. It represents where our beliefs, feelings, and values are centered.

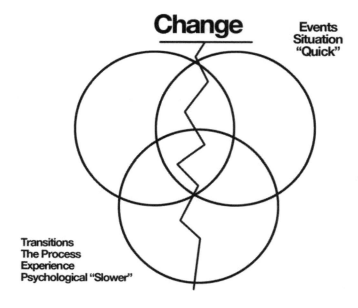

Outside events that cause unavoidable change cut through our core. They create a need for us to respond to the change through a personal transition process. Change impacts us immediately, which is a quick external process, whereas the Transition is an internal slower process and will take much longer—because things will not be the same—and Transition triggers the internal loss process, regardless of whether we deal with changes well or not. Change is external; transition is internal.

This third illustration presents the cyclical nature of transition. Change impacts us, which ends our previous way of life. That leads to transition, which I often refer to as "The Process." During this period, we experience loss and will need to make many sacrifices. We will be taken into a place of turbulence before finding smooth air, then we gradually move from confusion about our circumstances to understanding. New insights allow us to move toward acceleration and take off for a new beginning, which eventually becomes the new way of life . . . until change strikes again (as it inevitably will—now at an even faster pace since rapid change is now a part of our culture) and we enter a new repetition of the cycle. However, hopefully each time we go through this transformation of change-to-transition-to-new-life, we gain in maturity and wisdom and can be more intentional and wise in our next round of processing. My actual experience of this is that each change brings new challenges and loss. We *will* be confronted again and again. However, we are called to surrender. This surrender or release is similar to Jesus in the Garden of Gethsemane when he asked the Father to take this cup of suffering away but ultimately released his will and said, "your will be done" (see Matthew 26:39). There are no shortcuts on this journey; then we, like Jesus, will be allowed to see glory.

Because change and transition create temporary imbalance and discomfort in individuals undergoing major change in their church, we would do well to provide them with support during this time. Although the senior leader-pastor is not likely to be the appropriate person to take this role—as he or she must concentrate on steering the plane—designating a crew member to facilitate careful and caring listening would be a compassionate, effective way to ease the turbulence and pain of change. This congregational-care crew member, chosen by the pilot-pastor leader and equipped to serve the body, would listen, however many times as necessary, to the angst and grief of congregants, providing an opportunity to guide them throughout the process into a deeper walk with Christ. This qualified crew member or the copilot, both of whom are equally committed to the mission, could be a powerful conduit to the pilot, providing effective caring while feeding back critical information on the condition of the body during the flight. This process will allow the pilot-pastor to keep a steady course and conduct flight plan briefings with the crew and passengers at regular intervals.

Listening, Hearing, and the Power of Our Words

Listening—*really* hearing and listening—is absolutely key to helping people find their way through personal transitions that inevitably emerge in the course of change, transition, and transformation. Listening is critical to communicating vision and compassionate care during time of loss and conflict. We cannot—do not—move forward well without listening.

I saw this principle in action recently when I was involved in a group conversation. A man asked one of the women members, a mom, how her daughter was doing in finding a college. The woman responded that her daughter had graduated and was looking at a prestigious college in New York City. The man replied by saying, "You have my condolences."

The mother's facial expression changed, her eyes grew wide, and she said, "Oh? Why do you say that?"

He said, "Well, it's going to be quite expensive."

"Oh," she said. "I know that, but she will be getting paid as an intern." I was thinking, *New York City is such an enormous, scary place.*

I said, "Are you worried about your daughter being in such a big city alone?" Tears welled up in her eyes as she nodded. It was only through observing and listening between her words that we were able to talk about the real issue that was troubling her.

To be heard is to be validated. We can find smoother air of ministry and give ourselves a lift by listening and hearing better.

Hear Plus *Art* Equals *Heart*

Visionary leaders will often be very excited and far ahead of most people in their personal processing of transitions. Thus, they often make the mistake of not stopping to listen to validate others' feelings in regard to their loss. When leaders listen, that does not mean change will *not* occur. It may not occur as fast as the leader would like, but the process will be much more civil.

When people are asked to make behavioral changes in something they hold as dear to them as the church, there will be a need to be heard. We can do them and ourselves a great service by offering them the gift of listening and being heard. Listen with empathy without being defensive and give validity to their feelings. This will make our journey and theirs a much smoother one. The change process can then proceed with less resistance, perhaps with more cooperation and support.

If we are to minister with compassion—and systemic change will present many such opportunities—we must develop the art of hearing from the heart. I recently read an excellent article by Dr. Mort Orman.[3] He speaks of the following seven keys to better listening skills (the thoughts in italics are mine).

1. Listening is NOT a passive activity! *We need to be fully present and engaged.*

2. Listen for unspoken fears, concerns, moods, and aspirations. *This is "heart listening," and will help in our planning processes.*

3. Good listening requires great wisdom. *Wisdom is often referred to in Scripture as a woman or as Fe-male. Proverbs give us abundant resources here.*

31

4. Listen to others with respect and validation. *Sometimes a simple thank-you is needed and is enough to recognize the contributions people have made.*

5. Listen without thinking about how you're going to respond.

6. Listen for tell-tale signs of impending trouble. *This will prove helpful in guiding the change process. (We'll read accounts in the later chapters where people say things that have important messages "underneath." Listening between the lines often averts problems.)*

7. Listen with positive regard for people's strengths and abilities. *This will be helpful in placement for future ministry positions and gifts of the church.*

To really hear someone, we have to attend to background messages, the unspoken emotions and concerns. This takes time and attention. However, many leaders refuse to slow down long enough to actually listen. It's like being in such a rush to take off in a blizzard that we don't deice the plane; it will distort our perspective and eventually shut down the system, if not make the plane crash! But when we do hear people, we can give them feedback and eye contact that allow them to know that they have been heard—*really* heard. This validation is often all that is needed. They need to know that what they are expressing matters.

If, for example, your church has gone through a past split and traumatic conflict and now has been calm for a while, the mention of change will not necessarily come with glad tidings. They may say that they really would like to talk to you about the music, the new paint color, whatever. The issue is not the issue. (By the way, alterations in music, décor, and paint are not considered systemic change issues. They are only surface issues to prepare for the real change that needs to take place.) If we can hear the *background* message, they may actually be voicing their unspoken concern that they don't want a repeat of the last painful situations that led to broken relationships. Or, they are feeling very out of control, and this is the only place where they can exert control.

If we immediately dismiss them as being against the change and resistant, we will miss the opportunity to hear their legitimate concerns, understand their fears, and encourage them while communicating the benefits of the change. Otherwise, they feel unheard and "bulldozed." If we fail to listen, why should we be surprised if some people rise up with a barrier of resistance that complicates and stalls the systemic change process?

We can also listen with an ear for impending problems or trouble on the horizon. People will generally allude to underlying concerns, and they have growing displeasure with some aspect of the relationship. They might not come out and say directly, but they expect us to interpret their cues and take some kind of action as a result. It is better to attend to this sooner than later. It is part and parcel to managing "the grapevine."

Compassionate Listening and the Church Transformation Process

Grief and loss are core concerns in a turnaround church setting. Hearing with a sensitive ear, good listeners have the ability to listen to people constructively and compassionately, despite the immediate pain being expressed.

We can listen to people communicate about a tragedy with a great deal of compassion. We can also listen with eyes to see their true inner strengths and inherent capabilities. We can remind them by letting them know how capable and courageous they are, even in the face of such terrible tragedy, and that in their weakness, God is strong. It may not lessen the pain, but it can give hope and encouragement. The Scripture teaches us to mourn with those who mourn and rejoice with those who rejoice. By listening attentively, we can do this. The person expressing tragedy will appreciate this gesture of love and support.

I remember clearly after the death of my son, a longtime acquaintance walked up to me to express her sympathy. She said to me, "I know just how you feel because I lost my cat." At the time, I was incensed at the comparison of her cat and my only son's death. Looking back now, I realize that what she was really trying to do was connect with me and to say how sorry she felt. And her cat was the closest thing to her that she had ever had to part with.

Listening about losses is essential to transformation—we need to remember that the transition of systemic change starts with people losing something—influence, control, significance. Future growth relies on past contributions and sacrifices. Sometimes a simple thank-you is enough to acknowledge what the organization's members have already given.

PART TWO

Making It to Mach 1

CHAPTER THREE

JOURNEY THROUGH TIME

Defining the Problem Determines Possible Solutions

In any daunting challenge, defining the problem is critical to finding practical solutions. So, when "they" labeled the task of transforming 220 declining and dying churches from declining and dying in a denomination that was also declining and dying as impossible, Paul Borden saw a different problem. But it wasn't what you might think. Paul really thought, *It is possible—through God*. He had the vision and found ways to approach the task of creating systems of transforming and systemically changing churches. But first he had to define the problem differently. Paul found that plateaued or declining churches function within a cluster of possible modes of operation—all of them dysfunctional in their own ways, all with topsy-turvy dynamics.

Before the invention of the airplane, there were naysayers.

"A man-carrying airplane will eventually be built, but only if mathematicians and engineers work steadily for the next one to ten million years" (*New York Times* editorial, 1903).

"Man will fly, but the craft will be the size of a matchbook and carry an insect for a passenger" (Simon Newcomb, a respected scientific authority, 1903).

Meanwhile, Wilbur Wright, a bicycle maker, said in 1900: "It is my belief that flight is possible."

What was it about the Wright brothers, working essentially on their own without benefit of a higher education or formal scientific and technological training, that enabled them to solve a problem so complex and demanding as heavier-than-air flight, in only a few short years, with few funds, when it defied better-known experts for centuries?[1] What characteristics did they possess that we need now?

There were many reasons for the Wright brothers' success. One was that they correctly defined stability and control as their starting point. Prior attempts at flying involved erratic swerves, nosedives, and the inability to hold altitude. Most of the contraptions never got off the ground! Other engineers and scientists defined the problem as one of power and speed, thinking if they had enough power and speed, they would handle the control and stability issues after they got the flying machine in the air. But in reality, the control and stability issues kept them from getting the machine in the air in the first place.

Since the Wright brothers were looking at a different problem, their minds were prepared for a different solution. One day, a lightweight box with bicycle inner tubes arrived at their shop. Wilbur happened to pick it up in such a way that it twisted and warped, but then went back to its regular shape. The idea struck him of a warped wing instead of a flat wing that day, and it was not much longer until this new kind of wing lifted an airplane aloft for a stable, controlled flight!

So, Wilbur and Orville Wright were able to create a different future because they defined a different problem to solve. Half a century later, President John F. Kennedy would build upon the Wright brothers' ideology and lead a nation to stratospheric results: "The problems of the world cannot possibly be solved by skeptics or cynics, whose horizons are limited by the obvious realities. We need men [and women] who can dream of things that never were."[2]

Whatever the story line of declining churches in need of transformation, embedded deep in the plot is a basic lack of trust, which causes the similar kinds of control and stability issues that prevented early airplanes from flight. All of these things can also wreak havoc on the self-worth and value of both the pastor and his spouse.

Many male pastors, like most Christians, gain much of their significance from their work or ministry. When congregations fail to grow, pastors see themselves as the problem. In some cases that is true, while in many cases few if any pastors could lead certain congregations for transformational change without expert help. Often the pastor's self-worth declines and impacts his marriage. A wife can either become codependent in trying to help her husband or angry when her mate seems incapable of producing change. Most often a woman finds a sense of fulfillment and satisfaction in connecting and relationships. When trust is broken and power exerted, all relationships will suffer. However, when hope is introduced, the hope of a healthy congregation will bring hope to the marriage as well.

It is really imperative to have a basic understanding of the problem because until the power and trust issues are taken care of the leadership will be under attack. There will still be other challenges, even if power and trust issues are resolved.

It is as if a group of passengers take over the cockpits and air-traffic controls because no one else is there. In this situation, the pilot casually boards the plane and sits in the economy class, instead of sitting up front. It is as if the pilot says, "Where are we heading today? Hope it's a good flight. Hope we get there." The "leader" is passive; so, in reaction, the "followers" take over, forcing perilous directions that can lead to a nose-dive—or worse: crashing and burning.

Or, in another scenario, congregants get aboard the airplane but are really only there for the entertainment, comfort, and service. They're consumers, focused primarily on their own destinations and plans without regard for others waiting to board or the flight crew.

Or, in an even more radical (but unfortunately realistic) scenario, some aboard the flight turn out to be emotional terrorists who hold people hostage with threats, lies, and betrayals. Sometimes they are like snipers who try to shoot down every new and good idea because "we've never done it that way before." As ammunition, they use innuendo, criticism, faultfinding, gossip, threats to withhold their giving, and so forth. Sometimes they are triangulators, involving a third party in their disputes without ever having discussed their issues with the first party. Sometimes they form resistance groups and get a critical mass of people galvanized against the changes taking place.

We can see all too clearly the damage that is being done in our world today as a result of rogue operatives; it's no different in our churches, as the following story from a real Woman Married to a Man in Transformational Ministry so poignantly describes.

Giving Voice 3
Initiating Change in a Church We Already Lead

It is hard to think back to when the voyage really began. The point of conception for me was at a leadership prayer meeting.

Executive Minister Paul Borden had been to the church, and a leadership group of about twenty-five people met to examine his findings. We began to cast the vision that those findings inspired. The level of excitement in the room rose as people shared their dreams for the future of the church. Suddenly, we were all kneeling beside our chairs and praying for God's will to be a guiding light for the future. We prayed for courage and willingness to risk for what God wanted to do with our church.

I think my husband and I foresaw a great adventure. We prepared with excitement and boarded the plane of change with a little pride that we were able to venture out. We took our seats, buckled up, and then . . . our plane was hijacked! We did not go where we intended. We visited many destinations we did not plan on. We often felt we had a gun to our heads. Fear was our constant companion. We have not reached our intended destination yet. The ride is still bumpy and fearful. We still lose a passenger here and there. We will probably never fly again with the careless abandon of the past, but we still think the destination will be reached.

The first big step was literally packing our bags to move out. The decision was made to sell our one-acre piece of property and the building that many of those still active in the church had built and paid for. The vote was to be held on a Sunday morning after the service. The proposal was made and questions or statements from the floor opened. One older person stood and said that what we were doing was disrespectful and hurtful to those who had died. They had gone to the church at this site and it was not fair to them to move it. Many spoke in favor of the move, and the final vote passed with little dissent.

We did not take seriously the comment about offending the dead, for our concern was for the living and most of those seemed excited about the vision for growth in our region and a new location and better facility. Looking back, we should have heard between the lines. That elderly man was not as concerned with the dead as with himself. We were pushing him out of the place that was comfortable and familiar, and that lone, small voice was to become an outcry as we traveled along our way.

We began naively looking for land. We thought this would be an easy project. We held a capital campaign and many pledged. I can remember standing at a former shopping mall with a group of leaders plus a minister from our area who was kind enough to come and share his expertise. The mall was up for sale. The facilities offered some unique possibilities for ministry, retreats, and gatherings. We were seriously considering it, and our expert said he was amazed we had a congregation willing to step out in such a unique way. How we misunderstood the level of commitment that change demands! The deal fell through, and then began three years of searching and unending questions from church members who felt we should have had a new building within a year, two at the most.

We do have more than thirty acres now, bordering the land we first found. God had something better for us. God also provided a new facility, where we continue to meet on Sundays, with setup and teardown as a weekly project. We continued working through the county hoops to get our land approved for building.

The vision for outreach was still alive and well. Large events were held that would attract people to church—concerts, fun nights, worship events, women's events. From each we gained new members, but something startling was happening to our members. They no longer knew everybody in church, and this was uncomfortable. Many of the new people did not look the way they thought church people should. Tattoos, piercings, jeans, cutoffs, wild hairdos and clothes—this was not what "growth" should look like.

Gradually we missed seeing this person, then that family, then another. First, it was the older members. Our service just didn't feel like church anymore. The auditorium was not like the church, the sound was not as good, the music was different, the chairs were not padded pews. "Could we please sing the old hymns," was a resounding cry. Once the praise team leader jokingly said if someone wanted hymns, they should write it on a note and maybe attach it to a $50 bill. The next Sunday I put in a $50 bill with "Great Is Thy Faithfulness" on an attached note.

I am a "people pleaser," and I was desperate to please people. The people we had ministered to for more than twenty-five years were unhappy. Our children had grown up with their children. My husband had married, buried, and baptized members of these families. With our personal families far away, these people had been our family. Now, they were dissatisfied about so many things—things they had been part of setting in motion.

Most left the church without a word. When we realized they had not been coming, we went to visit. So many hard visits. They cried, said they loved us and missed us, but the church changed and was not meeting their needs anymore; they were not comfortable, the church wasn't like it had been when we were growing up.

After each of these visits my husband and I would be an emotional disaster, feeling sick, exhausted, and beaten. We were consumed at times with self-doubt. I was worse than my husband. Despite all the turmoil, he still clearly felt that the purpose of the church must be changed from being a place to primarily comfort and encourage believers into being a place to reach out and rescue a dying generation.

I was terrified of the new change! Before long, I begged my husband not to do it. We fought at times because he was set on a course and I couldn't face the cost! I couldn't stand to lose anyone else. To his credit, he loved me and was there for me but was not deterred, and to my credit, after throwing a fit, I came alongside and gave it my all. That giving began to take a toll on me.

People would come to me with their complaints, because I was more sympathetic and would listen. They felt my husband would not listen, because when they gave him ultimatums to change this or that, he listened but would not make changes opposed to the purpose of the church. I would do everything I could to be all things to all people, no matter the cost. I gave countless parties, created groups to get people connected: home builders, twenty-year-olds, motorcycle riders, a senior adult ministry, Awana. You want it? I'll do it!

With my full-time work position, and one of these activities once each month, every day of my life was fully taken. I traveled as fast as I could, and one day I hit a wall. Then people went after my son. As a mother, you can do what you want to me, but don't touch my baby! Our son was the youth minister at church and had done an amazing job for several years during and after college. He put his heart and soul into ministry and, into all of these people's children. They loved him, but when they left the church, their kids left with them, and the vital youth group that he had nurtured took an awful hit. He was blamed.

Watching this program hurt; I began to lie awake at night desperately wanting to escape. Our Bible study group that had been together for two years pulled apart; I had no support group; I was tired and got up less and less often at 5:00 a.m. to do my Bible study and prayer time before work. When I got home at 6:00 p.m. I had group meetings and homework. I was too tired to do Bible study.

My husband was doing several studies, but for the first time I stayed home, so my spiritual life spiraled downward. I dreaded going to church. By Friday, I came home from work ready for the weekend, but soon after getting home began to fear Sunday coming. By Sunday morning I was literally sick—Sunday after Sunday. One day, I just wanted to die.

I comforted myself in bed thinking of ways to die that would not look like suicide. Sounds crazy, I know. I'm not usually a wimp, but I could not face life. I heard an ad on the radio for a ministry for pastors who were burned out. I asked my husband about it, but he said he was not burned out. I told him I was, I really needed to talk to someone, and I had learned long ago never to say anything to anyone in the church, unless I was willing for it to be broadcast on Sunday morning.

I needed to be able to unload all of this garbage that had become excess baggage somewhere safe. My husband made the appointment, I met with a counselor who wanted me to come weekly, but that cost over a hundred dollars a session. It only added to my stress. I gave it up. I'm pretty tight, always looking for deals, and at those rates, I decided I had to pull myself together and get on with it. I started getting up again and began at Genesis, going through the Bible, studying and praying.

We started up a new Bible study in my home after doing Saddleback's "40 Days of Community." The group had new people and old people. A great mix. The new people shared how wonderful the church was, how it had changed their lives, brought families back together, made fathers whole again. God gave me the best group possible. This was our vision, but I had been so focused on problems, hurts, and disappointments, that I missed seeing that God had been working miracles in the lives of those people I greeted each Sunday morning with a hug.

News came in the mail, from the most unexpected people, telling me how the church had helped them, how God was real to them now, and even how I was an example to them. Me! As I spiraled downward, God lifted me upward so gently that I didn't even know it. I'm not sick on Sunday mornings anymore. I still hurt over those we've lost. I still cringe when I get invited to baby showers, wedding showers, weddings, and birthday parties for all those people who've left. They still call my husband to do the weddings and funerals, saying that even though they go to church somewhere else, he is still their pastor. Someday, I'll laugh about that, but not yet!

Long, long ago, before we ever began this journey, God almost audibly spoke to me. I can't explain it, I just heard it. He said, "Don't focus on the loss, keep your eyes on the goal." I didn't really know what that meant at the time. Now, I know exactly what it meant. I take it as a warning and a promise. We will reach the goal. The joy in ministry comes in moments of awe. It's not the constant that it was for many years of ministry, but maybe it's more precious, for I see its rarity and value now. I see that God's purpose will be accomplished when we as a church body all race enthusiastically together, but also when we go kicking and fighting.

This last Sunday, my husband spoke on one person reaching out to share Christ with another, and that person reaching out and touching another, and as he did he asked those to stand and connect in the line, and then someone to come and join in. In a matter of moments, the entire church body was one large circle of people standing together, holding hands, expressing their desire to be used by Christ to reach another. Wow! What a high! As I stood looking around the circle and hundreds of people, new and old, ready to touch our world, joy flooded my soul.

It's funny, but I find encouragement in the story of Moses wandering in the desert. Our church is in the desert, and like Moses, my husband and I are getting old and may never be a part of ministry in the new church building. But also like Moses, God is letting us see from the top of the hill that his will is going to be accomplished. I hang on to several verses that get me through the hard days. "Be still, and know that I am God" (Psalm 46:10). Spending time with God is better than spending time venting with anyone else. Satan will never want our church to change, and he will fight us every inch of the way, but "the one who is in [us] is greater than the one who is in the world" (1 John 4:4).

I am a very tidy person, and I want everything done immediately. God's timing is not my timing. Our Bible study group is going through Genesis. We're all seeing this familiar book as if it were brand-new. Abraham is our hero. He had to wait on God's promise until it seemed impossible, until it was only possible through God's hand and not through any natural manner. Our church building will be built, our people will make an incredible mark for Christ on our community, and his praises will be raised by his people, because in my mind (though not totally in my heart), I believe it is not what my husband and I do, but what God does that will make the difference.

Describing Effects of the Problem on Women

Ministry at its best is difficult, but when you launch systemic change processes, the challenge multiplies by the power of ten. Change in ministry approaches and systems evokes transitions in personal life and family systems; for example, the pastor and the woman married to him must realize that no real change will come without pain. If they, like Jesus, are not ready for a cup of suffering, they, like him, would never see glory. In this case their glory is leading a healthy growing congregation while having a healthy family relationship as they are obedient to the Great Commission. Once we launch into moving a church into Great Commission focus and church health, both system change and personal transition are *inevitable*. The issue becomes how do we navigate them?

For ten years now I've had a bird's-eye view and watched one woman after another deal with radical change and transitions. They have approached these in various ways and means. Some were more adventurous than others but only a very few glided through the experiences. Others felt like they were on the battlefield, some on a free fall without a parachute, and still others took skydiving lessons and prayed that their parachutes would open. Many had "transformational acrophobia" and were afraid of flying through change altogether. The fear of flying can cause panic attacks and high levels of anxiety. If they do not receive support, help, and relief, it can destroy their health at worst and keep them grounded, never allowing them to know the heights that they could reach. Sometimes the help and support that is needed may be a safe listening ear of someone who has experienced their plight and flight. In other cases it might require professional counseling.

Knowing and caring for these women, seeing them going through difficulties or even devastation, is a painful process for me, to say the least. If we are going to continue in a successful ministry and take it to Mach-10 levels, we must find another way. We must have the resources to do so.

I'd like to take a closer look at change and transition first, then consider ways and means for us to better navigate these components of the transformation process.

Transformation and Agents of Transformation

We serve a changeless God, yet life with Christ is a transformation full of changing circumstances, and our growth transitions in response. If we are changing, there is a good chance that we are growing, and if we are growing according to biblical descriptions, then we are being transformed into the image of Christ, even when the change is painful.

The Scriptures are replete with the language of change, such as being transformed, born again, putting off the old and putting on the new (2 Corinthians 4:7-16; Ephesians 4:25–6:11). Still, within ourselves we must find a solid and secure core of unchangeableness, plus an outward pliability that allows us to trust in God and move ahead, even when it seems counterintuitive. The apostle Paul has taught us, but like Christ, the path to glory always goes through the land of suffering (Romans 8:17). If we are called to follow Jesus, we must know that we are called to walk the same path.

Transformation, Change, Transition

I realize that life is full of the unexplainable and the unexpected. Life has taken many odd turns, none of which I could have anticipated. It seems like changes in circumstances sometimes come out of left field. One day everything is just fine, life as usual, and the next thing you know your spouse files for divorce, the real-estate bubble bursts, you lose your job, your child dies. I have experienced all these things. As I did, I felt as if I'd been hit in the stomach and kicked in the back of the knees at the same time.

Other times, new circumstances may be something more positive, like a wonderful job promotion. However, then you need to move across the country, leaving family and friends and support systems behind. Or perhaps you've just been given news that you're having twins and you already have three other children.

Change touches us all, and as it does, it tests. It tests our faith. It tests what we're made of, our true core being. Our responses to changes in circumstances bring us to personal transitions. Change does not automatically translate into growth, but when we align our responses with God's plans, our transitions bring transformation.

When we're facing a big change, whether it's at a deep personal level, or at home, work, or church, we want to know why it's happening and how it's going to affect us. In the case of church change, most people want to know "what's in it for me?"

Ways and Means for Change and Transition

Decades ago, Dr. Wernher von Braun stated that the natural laws of the universe are so precise that we do not have any difficulty today building a spaceship, sending a [person] to the moon, and calculating the timing for the landing with the precision of fractions of a second. And yet, the exploration needed within the "inner space" of the human heart seems harder to reach than outer space, with far less precision and predictability. (Von Braun understood that the problem was not in the science of the rocketry. The problem is in its implementation and chance of human error and or faulty materials.) There are intriguing comparisons and contrasts here that illuminate the issues of change and transition.

In outer space, there is no atmospheric pressure and no oxygen to sustain life. Temperatures range widely between extreme hot and cold, and seemingly innocuous floating particles can actually inflict severe damage. Inside the spacecraft, all of these factors can be controlled. But in order to explore and work outside the spacecraft, human beings must take a portable, sustainable environment with them. They need the specialized protection, insulation, and supplies of a space suit.

The exploration of "inner space" requires just as much attention in order to sustain life and growth. For inner-space work, the Scriptures talk about putting on the armor of Christ (Ephesians 6:10-17). This important spiritual protection enables us to withstand the heat and attacks caused by change and transition. While this is not new information to most of us in ministry, I fear we don't take its importance seriously enough.

We'll continue to explore the idea of inner-space work as we examine principles that move us toward Mach-10 ministry.

CHAPTER FOUR

FLIGHT PLAN

Shuttle Launch: Insulation for Our Identity

As I was watching the shuttle launch on July 4, 2006, the announcer talked about the importance of the "heat shield," the protective covering around the shuttle to insulate it as it reenters the atmosphere. That is how I see this book. It provides insulation as women begin to find their voice and create their unique position of service in the church, and, with that, find the freedom to soar.

There will be a great deal of resistance pushing against the wind of change. Each woman will need a gravity-defying level of confidence of who she is in Christ and confidence in herself to make decisions outside of cultural norms. Women in ministry and Women Married to Men in Ministry are redefining ministerial stereotypes and leading in new ministry approaches. While women have traditionally been socialized to please authority figures such as parents and teachers, and sometimes pastors, they often feel pressured to fulfill the expectations others hold for them. However, these "new paradigm" women know through intuition and experience that being true to yourself and your understanding of God is one of the greatest gifts we have to share. This is an important truth. It will help empower and strengthen us as we practice telling our truth and sharing it; it will serve as a model for those who will follow us. These are often hard-learned lessons while on the front lines of the war of change.

The flight is not a woman's only flight. It will require a whole support system, a whole new crew, and a whole new framework of tools.

Our transport vehicles will be a healthy marriage and a healthy church. As Joe Aldrich says in his classic book *Lifestyle Evangelism*,

> The two are interdependent. You can't have one without the other. It is the healthy marriage, however, that is the "front line weapon." A Christian family in a community is the ultimate evangelistic tool, assuming the home circle is an open one in which the beauty of the Good News of the gospel is readily available. It is the old story where love is seen [and, I would add, experienced], the message is heard.[1]

A healthy marriage is one where two emotionally healthy people respect each other, value the gifts God has given to each, and choose to focus on that which is best in the other person. Marriage begins with romance. Romance is that sprinkle of magic that comes when each partner is so enthralled with the talents, personalities, and gifts of the other that they move from deep respect and honor to love. However, no romance can be sustained without the biblical agape, which comes from the will to focus in on that which is true, noble, right, pure, lovely, admirable, excellent, or praiseworthy in the other person (Philippians 4:8).

No one is perfect nor meets another's needs all the time. Therefore, healthy marriages are where the partners focus more on each other's goodness than their foibles. The problem with most young couples, including men who are pastors and women married to them, is that they are more concerned about how their spouse treats them than how they treat their spouse. Health comes in the relationship as they move away from having their needs met to meeting the needs of their spouse. The challenge is the living-out in daily life this description of marriage. To become emotionally healthy is not automatic and cannot be assumed. We all have the emotional baggage that needs to be unpacked, and if the relationship has been challenged by broken trust, adultery, neglect, or abuse along with any other of life's major traumas and day-to-day challenges of living, this packing and unpacking process will be painful, time-consuming, and necessary.

We certainly will need to be committed to God's word and submit our thought life to him on a daily basis as we navigate the atmosphere of daily relationships in order to have our thinking aligned with his word. Service to each other in a spirit of love without malice—yes, even after that horrendous argument—will take both determination and courage.

Some of the most thoughtful and in-depth work I have read on the subject of marriage is written by Alice Mathews and M. Gay Hubbard in their book *Marriage Made in Eden: A Pre-Modern Perspective for a Post-Christian World*. The book is about marriage, but it is about marriage that takes seriously the biblical mandate to live out a radical alternative in the present culture, which, despite its rhetoric, gives little evidence of loyalty to the true living God.

A *Newsweek* article entitled "The Heart of the Family," honoring the late Ruth Bell Graham, tells of her many sacrifices in service to God, her husband, and her family as she struggled through loneliness and depression as a young woman. Billy Graham expresses his love for his partner of sixty-four years. He describes their marriage as "happily incompatible," full of tenderness and friction. Ruth saw her role as one to both challenge and support her husband, and she did so unflinchingly.

I certainly can relate to Ruth's story regarding the loneliness and isolation of this position as a Woman Married to a Man in Ministry. Paul and I are both leaders with strong opinions and very different perspectives and personality styles. Opposites attract and repel, so it creates somewhat of a backdraft for turbulences and smooth air, making for a bumpy ride that requires your seat belt to be fastened. It's rarely a boring or uneventful flight, and we're always thankful for a safe landing.

It could be said that the good news is more caught than taught. In fact, the ancient wisdom most often attributed to St. Francis of Assisi says it best, "Preach the gospel at all times and when necessary use words." The cross is the mainstay to all points above and beyond, and healthy ministering couples modeling the way are critical to the launch.

But what exactly goes into preparation for launching a paradigm shift and systemic change in a congregation? In this chapter, we'll look at key aspects of what goes into a wholistic flight plan and how to deal with "turbulence" that occurs along the way. We'll also hear stories from ministry couples whose journeys have ended up as "connecting flights" with others in the process of church transformation leadership.

Sketching a Flight Plan: Bull's-Eye Principles for Where We Are Going

Flight plans require us to answer various who, what, when, where, why, and how kinds of questions about getting to our destination. Otherwise, we will end up hitting something—but it won't be the target we intended! Here is a sketch of a transformational church flight plan.

Where are we going? We want to lead this congregation to be qualitatively "healthy"—radically focused on the Great Commission and equipped mentally, emotionally, spiritually, and relationally to carry it out. While we will still minister to those in the current congregation, we will ultimately orient the church more toward those who are not currently part of us. This emphasis on outreach requires growing disciples in their relationship with God and in using their gifts for the kingdom.

Who is going? Some people on this flight are leaders, but everyone on board needs to participate in fulfilling the Great Commission. Since leadership is not only a gift but a practice, it is accessible to everyday disciples. Many people in the congregation can become leaders in significant system changes. Transformational change in turnaround churches begins with focusing on healthy leaders—women and men—and ensuring they maintain healthy families if they are married or have children.

Healthy families, like healthy marriages, are ones in which children are respected, honored, and loved in a sacrificial way. One of the ways we can honor, respect, and love our children is to make sure to set our priorities and schedule times with them daily for connecting and interacting; otherwise, it is very easy for them to feel that they are playing second to the church in importance. They must experience being with parents for quality time on a regular basis. However, unlike the behavior of many families today, healthy families do not teach children to be more important than the family. Through the establishment of boundaries, discipline, and other means, children are taught to be responsible for their choices. It is helpful for children to know we also personally accept the responsibility of our choices and also ask the members of the church to do so as well. Wise parents realize that the book of Proverbs teaches that their role is to help children stop foolish thinking and behavior in order that they may grow up in wisdom. Children learn from our doing more than our saying.

How do we get there? Transformational change requires our willingness to change any organizational structure that inhibits us from succeeding in our biblically mandated outward-looking mission. It also requires biblical accountability for both leaders and members—no hijacking allowed! So, we must resist whatever (or whoever) leads to or maintains a dysfunctional status quo, and we must focus on biblical means to develop whole, healthy Christians as agents of change.

What do leaders look like? Some critical characteristics for transformational leaders include: courage, flexibility, missional mind-set, wisdom, positive outlook, risk-taking, and responsibility. It involves purposeful passion that motivates us to action and passion like Christ's where embracing pain and suffering is meant for something larger. Good leaders constantly raise up new leaders and develop leadership traits in others. This reproduction is essential to implanting quantitative and qualitative growth.

What could get in the way? There are at least five general barriers to turnaround change for churches to become the missional enterprises that Jesus Christ both modeled and commanded:

1. Many men in ministry do not see themselves as leaders of congregations, except perhaps in the spiritual realm, accepting the title and role of "spiritual leader." Many see their first responsibility being to the church, its leadership, and its protection—in lieu of the protection of their spouse and family.
2. Men in ministry have been conditioned to perform in an environment where "faithful endeavor" is honored but "fruitful results" are not expected or demanded—of themselves or their followers.
3. Many congregations are actually led by a handful of people who gained positions of control by default, in the absence of biblical leadership, and the result is a deterioration of the church system to conserving the status quo. They create "turbulence."
4. Church governance of many congregations in First World nations is designed in ways that keep churches small. These structures often allow dysfunctional people to control the congregation and stop change. They do not reproduce leaders; their inflexible cultural systems make them function ineffectively and irrelevantly in the twenty-first century.
5. The unrealistic expectations and ungodly scheduling result in burnout, often leading to personal attacks on the pastoral couple for not performing according to the status quo.

Unexpected Turbulence

My husband and I travel thousands of miles every year, both nationally and internationally. So we're accustomed to hearing the pilot's announcements to keep our seat belts buckled in case of unexpected turbulence.

Turbulence is a movement that normally cannot be seen. It can happen unpredictably, even when the sky appears to be clear. It can be created by any number of different conditions, including atmospheric pressures, jet streams, mountain waves, cold and warm air fronts, or thunderstorms.

Many passengers do not understand the causes or effects of turbulence or that it can occur without warning. The same holds true for anyone in a leadership position in ministry. If we're leaders for any length of time, we'll experience turbulence.

When we or our spouses make strategic changes and ask people to "change behaviors," there will be different intensities of turbulence. As a woman married to the Executive Minister of a judicatory that is initiating church change, I will continue to encounter turbulence.

When my husband's motives are under attack and being questioned, it brings stress. Often the stress brings us closer together, but it is still stressful. Since we believe that changes are needed, we keep pushing forward. We will not let the stress divide us. Turbulence sometimes comes part and parcel of getting to our destination.

We cannot afford to be flying by the seat of our pants; we need training and preparation, and then we need to fasten our seat belts. It also helps to consider the degrees of severity in atmospheric turbulence as they parallel our church context.

"Light turbulence" causes mild, erratic changes in altitude and attitude (that is, how the airplane is situated—upright, banking, rolling). This can be just the normal everyday jostling of personalities where we can observe the foibles, eccentricities, peculiarities, and just plain goofiness of our humanness.

In the change process, we regularly experience what's called **"light chop"**: slight, rapid, and somewhat rhythmic bumpiness without noticeable change in altitude or attitude. This is usually at the beginning of the change process when people are trying to figure out where they fit into the picture of the new vision.

"Moderate chop" is similar to light chop but with greater intensity. Rapid bumps or jolts hit us without obvious changes in altitude or attitude. This will happen when people start to figure out that change is no longer just a theory but will impact the way they do church. You will likely experience criticism, barbs, and complaints about why things can't be like they used to be.

During **"severe turbulence,"** we experience larger, broad changes in altitude and attitude. Large variations in air speed may cause the aircraft to be temporarily out of control. This is when people really *understand* that the changes will affect them personally, and they could lose their sense of significance, their ability to influence, and their position of power. This can be a very threatening and scary place to be! As a result, there will be attacks and character assassination beyond your wildest imagination.

"Extreme turbulence" is the most intense disruption of all. The aircraft is tossed about and is impossible to control. The intense shaking can actually cause structural damage, such as a stress fracture or a separation where the metal actually splits.

Inside the aircraft, the physical reactions to turbulence vary from passengers feeling slight strain against their seat belts and unsecured items being slightly displaced, to the occupants being forced violently against seat belts and unsecured items being tossed about. Now, just imagine what would happen to us if we were not wearing a seat belt! Extreme turbulence could throw us out of our seat and up against the ceiling of the aircraft, causing bodily harm and permanent damage. It would feel like we were in a battle!

Spiritually speaking, extreme turbulence can cause the church-change process to go out of control and into a downward spiral. This intense shaking occurs when a few people decide "We've never done it that way before, and we aren't about to change now." This will cause a "microburst"—a storm that starts a downdraft close to the ground and moves upward, hitting the pastor and his family. This microburst will often come from influential leaders. Nothing hurts quite as much as being wounded by one of your own. But, this is a reminder of just how fallen and in need of forgiveness we all are.

When we are aware that there will be many different kinds of turbulence, we can begin to prepare ourselves both emotionally and spiritually.

When more intense forms of "spiritual warfare turbulence" smack us around, we begin to question (if we haven't already) why we ever started this change process in the first place! This is the Mach-1 stage of violent shaking, just before breaking through the sound barrier. When we persevere, we *will* find smooth airspace—we *will* be able to minister in the way that we believed possible in the beginning of our journey.

I'm intrigued by what a friend of mine who is a jet pilot once told me: whenever a jet goes out of control and begins to spin, the only thing to do is totally take your hands off the controls and the plane will right itself. This goes against our natural inclination to control and manipulate in order to bring things back under control. It is scary to be out of control. Or is it? When we are in extreme turbulence, what does it mean to us that God *IS* the pilot?

Giving Voice 4
Entering a Church Already in Turbulence

God had called us to leave our church in order to serve in another congregation hundreds of miles away. And when I say "our," I mean it in the fullest sense of the word. This was the church where my husband and I had met, where we both became Christians, where we were married, and where our children had been dedicated. This was the church where my husband had served in ministry for twenty years, beginning as a part-time youth pastor, eventually becoming a full-time associate pastor. This was home.

I knew serving in a different church was God's desire, but that didn't make it any easier. I naively thought that leaving "life as we knew it" would be the most difficult part of the journey. Boy, was I ever wrong! It paled in comparison to the turmoil we would face with this new congregation. God said that the gates of hell will not stand against his church. Little did I know he was calling us to enter the gates to do battle.

Our new church was being torn apart from within. The interim period from when the previous pastor left until my husband came was very destructive. Three lay leaders had been left to run the church until their search committee found a new pastor. To say it didn't work well would be an understatement. During this time it became apparent that one of the lay leaders desired to become the pastor and another wanted his brother to pastor the church.

Added to the mix was a general distrust by some church members in the denomination's regional leadership assisting the search committee in finding potential candidates. The region was making a major paradigm shift on how to grow healthy churches, and the shift was attacked by some as being unchristian or unbiblical (a ludicrous argument). A few of the distrusting members were even on the search committee! The table was set for contention, disunity, and, if not corrected, the church's ultimate destruction.

Enter our little family! We were dropped into a war zone for which we weren't prepared. We expected the usual battles that

---

come with transition and leadership change, but this was covert warfare, everyone having chosen a side, yet on the surface all looking and acting the same. There was no uniform, no distinction, and no way to determine outright friend or foe—just little tremors (comments or behaviors) to indicate something wasn't quite right.

We didn't know it initially, but we had been assigned a "side" simply by coming to the church through the region. We were automatically suspect to many in the congregation, and anything my husband decided, said, or conveyed was seen through the veil of being unbiblical or soft theologically. He could have been Jesus himself and it wouldn't have mattered! We were aligned with the region, and the region was wrong. We were also wrong for the two lay leaders who desired someone else to be pastor.

As the turbulence grew over the next months, the shaking began to come to our attention in the form of rumors and gossip. Then it became attacks on my husband's character and integrity. The ripple effect from the turbulence increased to include me and anyone in support of my husband. People who were supposedly mature Christians dealt in innuendo and outright lies. Some even took part in secret meetings to make a list of demands regarding my husband's leadership and church policy. I couldn't believe what was happening. It was a spiritual struggle for power and control of God's church.

All I wanted to do was flee. All I could think about was the church and life we had left behind. I became severely depressed and experienced panic attacks and anxiety. I was filled with anger at our situation and the unjustness of it all. I wanted to stand up during church service to rail against those who were destroying this church and my family, yet I couldn't, so I railed at God. *Why? Why did you bring us here? Why do they hate us so? This isn't right. This isn't fair. Is saving this church the only thing you care about? Don't you care about what this is doing to me? Save the church and if I get destroyed in the process, oh well?* Satan seemed to be rejoicing at our plight.

The turbulence became most violent at the two-year anniversary of our ministry at the church. Believe me, I was in no mood to celebrate. I was physically, mentally, and spiritually exhausted. I was hurting for my family and for the church, God's church, the bride of Christ, which is supposed to be representative of his body. Our church was a sorry example. Disunity had the upper hand, and it was shaking our church to destruction.

At that two-year point there was a very ugly congregational meeting the Sunday before we were to leave on a family vacation. All covert warfare was abandoned. The sides came out in the open, confronting my husband's leadership and the direction of the church under the region's plan for Growing Healthy Churches. Though the majority of the congregation supported my husband, this band of disunity and selfishness was sustaining a destructive turbulence. When would it stop? During the meeting I gave God an ultimatum. Either these people are gone from our church when we return from vacation or I am. When we returned from vacation they were gone, leaving the church permanently. The turbulence had stopped. I rejoiced over the stillness and God's mercy.

It still took years for the church and my family to heal from the effects of the turbulence. We were all battle-weary and bruised. But God tenderly dressed our wounds, and with his grace and guidance, we endured and are now prospering. We have a healthy church. Our church and family walked through the turbulent gates of hell, but because of God's faithfulness, came out the other side victorious.

Author's Note: I wanted to include the postscript below to bring attention to the fact that even in recalling this experience after seven years, it is still a painful process and our connection and relationship with each other has been an important part of this process.

Postscript: Hi, Teresa—Well, here it is finally! I hope some of it is helpful for your book. Wow. Like you warned, this was hard. The bitterness is gone but the emotions are still strong when brought up. I am so looking forward to seeing you soon.

Turbulence-Causing People and Finding "Peace"

Mir is the Russian word for "peace." It was also the name of the Soviet space station. I have used the acronym M.I.R. to stand for My Inner Relationship. When relational troubles and turbulence assail us in our flight to transform our ministry, M.I.R. is the place we must first secure peace amid the pain.

The nature of suffering is part and parcel of daily living and is woven throughout Scripture. If we expected smooth sailing, it would be all the more painful when we suddenly got "jolted for Jesus"!

We have an expectation as Women Married to Men in Ministry to think of the church as friends or family. However, a more realistic view is that some congregants see us as friends, but many hold the attitude that *pastors and their families come and go and are there to serve as our employees*. So, the stories of church transformation leaders are full of situations where those they thought they could trust turned out not to be there for them when needed. Those they thought were friends became their worst critics. In reality, both the world and the church are filled with unsafe people. I have heard it said that there are three types of unsafe people: abandoners, critics, and the irresponsibles.

Everyone reacts to change and transition. So, it is very helpful to realize that when we as leaders become the lightning rods for people's reactions, these aren't really personal attacks, even though they feel that way. It helps to depersonalize the attacks when they start coming, to be able to back away and look at the big picture and not what is happening to us in the immediate circumstances. To help us get perspective and align with "true North," it is also very helpful to have trusted friends who are not directly related to the church in which we are leading change in ministry.

C. S. Lewis says, "God whispers to us in our pleasures . . . but shouts in our pain."[2] Pain is his megaphone to rouse a dulled world. If we allow it, the pain can be used to forge and form us into the image of Christ. Our perception of pain will also be a determining factor.

If we are convinced that it is God who has interrupted our lives by allowing turbulence, then we can keep our sanity. I have found in my own circumstance that the human spirit can withstand almost any tragedy if we can make sense of it or at least believe that God is in control. Jesus is the answer to our suffering. The realization of this, for me, has been a long process. Each person will find their own pace in which to work out their salvation.

It is here that we begin to ask if we really believe Romans 8:28: "All things work together for good." We must find a place of M.I.R.—a space of our own in which to connect to our Triune Spiritual Center: God the Father, God the Son, and God the Holy Spirit. They will be the calm in our storms and shakings. This will draw us closer to God and will draw us closer to others. It will help us to become the real person God created us to be through turbulent times.

CHAPTER FIVE

GETTING READY TO LAUNCH

Did Mr. Moses Have One Wife or Two?

Who remembers Mrs. Moses' name? How long was she in the picture anyway? Or did she virtually "disappear" when Moses went on his journey into "the ministry" there? Or was she always behind him, hidden?

Did she have boundaries prescribed around her? Was she on the sidelines all the time? or expected to always be in front of things? or remembered only for her outburst against him?

How did she deal with all the expectations, for this was the man chosen to release his congregation from bondage? Was she depressed? manic? tired? angry? frustrated? bored? sad? Did she suffer a crisis of neglect, or something worse, or not even know? Were there things she wanted to do, but could never get to?

Surely, there ought to be a law, but did her man have to be the one doing all the doing?

Moses eventually learned he could not do everything alone (Exodus 18:13-23).

Could Moses have accomplished God's mission for him without the sacrifices of his wife? And if she were here today, would she be in ministry? The Scripture really doesn't give us much information about the two wives of Moses. We know that his first wife, Tharbis, married during Moses' time in Egypt, was the daughter of an Ethiopian king. Some forty years later, his second wife, Zipporah, was the daughter of a Midianite priest, Jethro (Numbers 12). So we can only speculate that they did not spend a lot of time in the presence of their husband.

Women Married to Men in Ministry

For over three thousand years, some degree of separation from one's husband has been considered a normal part of being a Woman Married to a Man in Ministry. However, "normal" doesn't mean it is natural to us, or easy. In fact, it is one of the many sacrifices that go with the territory, part of being a servant in the body of Christ.

An intriguing tale is told in the Jewish Midrash (oral traditions) about Zipporah. It is set in the time when leaders are being chosen for the new nation of Israel:

> When the elders were appointed, all of Israel lit candles and rejoiced for them. Miriam saw the candles burning and asked Zipporah, "What are these candles for?" Zipporah told her.
>
> "Fortunate are the wives who see their husbands rise to high position," said Miriam.
>
> "Woe is to them," said Zipporah, "for henceforth their husbands will separate from them."[1]

Unfortunately, the role of Women Married to Men in Ministry has changed very little through the centuries. It's time to redesign this antiquated system, or life will remain the same for us and for our daughter generations who follow. Women of today need to discover healthy solutions for systemic change, thereby creating niches for themselves to serve out of who they truly are in Christ. For the sake of kingdom progress, Women Married to Men in Ministry must accept that the system will not change by itself. It is the women who must break down the barriers and select our own course of action and flight plan. After all, we, too, are personally called, gifted, and accountable for how we expend ourselves for the sake of the kingdom.

There is a difference between being a servant who ministers and being a slave. For too long, Women Married to Men in Ministry have worked within a faulty system of expectations that have tried to mold and form them into being all things to all people. Not only is that an exhausting job, it isn't one that anyone is called to! Add on to this the energy that must be expended by pastors, spouses, and ministry family members in trying to convince the church that *all is well* within their homes *all the time*. It is an impossible situation. And yet, such unreachable expectations still lurk within the church system, plus the expectations of the general public, of course. In conversations with people outside of the religious world, they generally hold ministers and their families to a higher standard than they themselves could live up to.

If a Woman Married to a Man in Ministry decides to play by the system rules, or feels forced to, she will experience an erosion of self and identity. As a result, she will be known as a "pastor's wife" and not as a woman in her own right.

We are all called by God. God wants all of us to be faithful disciples. However, the church has set apart a group of persons to serve God professionally, and some of these persons are pastors. A man's call into the profession of ministry is no higher a calling than a woman's call into professional ministry, or any other profession. God equips each of us uniquely for our calling so that we all have a part in bringing in God's kingdom. Just as God loves us all equally, God equips us each for ministry. It takes all kinds of people and their gifts to bring all kinds of people to Christ. And who are we to ask that anyone set aside his or her gifts when they are God-given. Might that make us like Peter when he objected to Jesus' plans to go to Jerusalem (Matthew 16:22-23)? Would Jesus also call us "Satan"?

During early conversations after my husband took over the role of Executive Minister in our judicatory, one woman spoke candidly with me. She said, "As a young married woman, I wouldn't have had the nerve or the knowledge to question the system or its expectations of me and my role in it. I would've thought it was the right way. I would've done as I was told, even if I didn't agree."

In my own youth, if I had been married to a man who was a pastor, I would've been more willing to limit myself and my horizons. I'm thankful that I entered the ministry arena later in life. Now that I've experienced more of life, I have the benefit of knowing myself and my strengths a lot better. I know that I'm not going to compromise myself. It has taken me many years to achieve and become the person that I am today. And, as a consequence, I believe that I have much more to offer in the communal life of the church.

Change happens one woman at a time. So, each woman must define for herself her own role as a Woman Married to a Man in Ministry. Otherwise it will be church politics as usual, and the anemic, stereotypical role of the "pastor's wife" will remain unchanged. The system will be inclined to respond to us as vital women only when we accept the challenge of exerting and expressing our influence and opinions, and expressing our needs both collectively and separately.

But husbands who are also pastors can help. They can be clear when congregants ask about us. They can volunteer, up front, that we have our own gifts and talents. Pastors can say not to be surprised if we don't help with Vacation Bible School (for example) or that we have interests and friends outside of the church. Pastors can say to congregants that we don't speak for them and don't carry messages to them.

If I'm "Just Supposed to Be Myself," Who Am I?

I've read various authors' advice to Women Married to Men in Ministry. They say "just be yourself." Sounds good, on the surface at least.

Just this very week I spoke with a forty-something Woman Married to a Man in Ministry. She said, "I have always been someone's daughter, someone's girlfriend, someone's wife, someone's mom. I've had the beliefs of my parents and now the beliefs of my husband. I really don't know who I am or what I believe." Sadly, this could be echoed a thousand times.

Yes, "just be yourself." But what I've discovered is that to *be* ourselves, we must *know* ourselves. I find that many women and men don't really know who they are. And most don't know who they are in Christ. A few lucky ones know early on who they are and what they want to do, but they are in the minority and perhaps haven't yet been refined by the fire.

I'm not sure that most people even begin to seriously ask the "who am I" questions until we are twenty or beyond, and if we're growing throughout our lifetime, we're still finding out answers when we are eighty. Most of us will go through some kind of refining fire during the process of finding self. We might feel jettisoned into space, a relatively unknown and uninhabited frontier, with no tether.

For some Women Married to Men in Ministry, the catalyst to a deeper sense of our true identity will come within the pressures of a dysfunctional church system, which can easily exacerbate issues of identity, anxiety, and betrayal. For some, it is the loss of health, loss of a job, memories of childhood abuse or neglect, or a crisis surfacing within their family of origin. Perhaps a move across the country is the catalyst or perhaps the disappointment of not being able to have a child, or deep-seated grief at the loss of a child, a home, creative input, our network and friendships, or recognition for our work.

Preparing to Fly

We can be sure that the Growing Healthy Churches process initiated by introducing systemic and transformational change will take us beyond anything we've experienced so far, in our life or in the life of our churches. Being a Woman Married to a Man in Ministry Leadership within the transforming church is a crucible that can forge growth. This process challenges everything we thought we knew about ourselves, our family systems, our friendships, and our Christian beliefs.

The mission of being obedient to the Great Commission takes us into enemy territory—it is serious business. As a Woman Married to a Man in Ministry, there really is no map and no route for us, just contrails in the dark cloudy sky. And just when we think that we understand the trajectory, recalculations will be needed, sometimes on a daily or weekly basis. This doesn't allow time to adjust to one change before the next is instituted. As a lifesaving measure we can learn to pack our own parachutes and then help someone else pack theirs; I am not speaking of bailing out, although there will be many times you will feel like bailing out. I'm talking about preparing yourself and others for a safe and softer landing. It's lifesaving in this wilderness frontier of space and time. Still, we may find ourselves disoriented, perhaps even disillusioned or depressed at times. But we are more than that.

Breaking the sound barrier is not about giving up or being a victim. It's about accepting that we're in transition ourselves and that we simply cannot know what's ahead. It's about whether we will become bitter or better. The process necessitates a willingness to be open to the unknown. It's about trust and when it's been built, broken, rebuilt. It is about risk and being transformed into the image of Christ, whatever the cost. It's about becoming ourselves as God always intended we should be.

Effecting Change in Kingdom Systems

My ten years of experience in the church world has left me with a cargo load of unanswered questions, a plethora of emotions, and always a burning curiosity of "What now?" and "Now what?" My intention in *Women Married to Men in Ministry* has been to present a multifaceted picture of who we are, where we fit into the system, and the parts we play as Women Married to Men in Ministry. Although some system changes depend on our unique situation, there are three basic changes we all can work on. I will describe these and then share stories of women who are effecting change.

1. Help Remove False Expectations and Stereotypes. The next giant "Now what?" step for Women Married to Men in Ministry is to determine what can be done to improve the church structure situation. It complicates matters that the church system has one set of expectations for Women Married to Men in Ministry and another for ministers themselves. Most women and men are put to the test each day by system stereotypes that lock them into certain limited modes of operation. These minimize their worldview and the parts they play in church change.

Thus, it appears that one way of impacting the system is for a woman to confront faulty rules and roles—with God's direction and empowerment, of course—and counteract them in ways that expose the toxic underlying expectations. If we want to make the system more healthy for ministry marriages and families, we as women need to initiate change and make modifications, with the support of our spouse and denominational leaders.

I find myself seeking to live by these words. I have owned my own businesses all of my adult life. I have served in many organizations, such as working with the AIDS Foundation and with Bridgeway, an organization for unwed teen moms and at-risk kids. I've had successful consulting and speaking careers, working with community colleges and corporate organizations. I now find myself in a nebulous role called "the executive minister's wife." But I refuse to let my plane sit on the runway—I confront some of the system flaws and fill in the gaps by maintaining my personal ministries for the kingdom and continuing my connections in the community.

2. Embody Wholistic Transformation Ourselves. In reality, since "the system" is composed of its people, and while only God can transform others, we as women in ministry can choose to change ourselves and our roles by being transformed into the image of God. What could it mean if we submitted every facet of our lives to Christlike transformation? That alone will bring a new set of dynamics into play!

Rather than complaining about the inequities of this life or suppressing any anger and frustration at "the system," we must be willing and fully prepared to change according to biblical terms, by choice. Since we are talking about change and transition processes in our church or judicatory, we must be ready to serve as role models ourselves by stepping up and taking charge of our own life transformation. We must maintain our balance and identity—that is, knowing ourselves as powerful, unique individuals. We must learn to strike the balance between our own needs as women and as Women Married to Men in Ministry, and between being separate individuals and coming together as one—another of God's many mysteries. We must become the change we want to see.

3. Create Safe Places of Support and Connection. While the pastor may have a support staff with which to engage and accomplish his goals and missions, it is the rare Woman Married to a Man in Ministry who has a support system. If Women Married to Men in Ministry are truly a priority and are seen as a viable contributing part of the ministry, then there must be allocations made to resource them and their needs, both in the local church and in the judicatory.

One thing I know for sure is that Women Married to Men in Ministry need a safe place to fall back on, a place for us to be ourselves—no questions, no strings attached, a place where we can take a deep breath and just be the woman God created us to be.[2] I experienced this kind of support system during the writing of this book. My coauthor Barbara, myself, and our project manager exchanged several hundred e-mails and many hours of phone calls and meetings during the four months of writing *Women Married to Men in Ministry*. In order to create this book, not all communication could be about this book. Life happened! We shared personal and family needs as prayer requests, processed what was going on in our lives, and encouraged one another on a regular basis. This happened spontaneously, and only near the final stages of writing did we realize that we had lived out the very thing we had talked about.

It seems this kind of connecting is rare. However, with my background and training in a paramedical day spa industry, it seems that I was born for such a time as this—to create such places of peace and refreshment, filled with color, light, and fragrance; a connecting place; a place of "In SPA Ration"; a center for the art and spirit of well-being, especially for women in ministry. Later, I'll share the story of "SPA Day," which became a significant marker in our judicatory's ministry among women. Meanwhile, the stories that follow dramatically illustrate the need for a safe, connecting, supportive place.

Giving Voice 5
Challenging Damaging Expectations: A "PK's" Story

Here are my memories as a "PK"—pastor's kid.

When my mom was a minister's wife in a rural community, we depended on the excess produce the congregational families brought since Dad's wages were so very small. Mom pretty much raised us alone since Dad was supposedly "called" to work twenty-four hours a day. There were five of us, so this was no small task. She learned to stretch that food—she must have been a genius or a genie, because all of us were nice and round—cute, but round. Also, she never made us feel poor. In fact, we didn't ever know we were poor until we were grown.

Mom has said many times that when congregations hired a minister they expected to get 2-for-1. She learned very quickly that if you said yes to doing something, you would pretty much do it forever. She soon came to resent the position she was in because she didn't choose it. When she married my father, she made him promise he would not become a minister. Well, when you are "called," I guess that overrides a promise. Dad couldn't see that there were other ways for God to use him.

Dad decided to be the dean of the church camp and took the whole family. I guess it was either that or Mom could stay home for a week or two with five children, so she went—we all went. My mother was not a camper! But she did fine under the circumstances, even though she is more of a city girl. I don't know if she was there every year, but I went to camp for ten years.

I remember going to church meetings and the shouting matches and criticisms of my dad, so I know Mom must have wanted to crawl under a pew. I learned that church people are human, too—and among the worst of them sometimes. Being put on a pedestal is something a minister chooses, but his wife does not necessarily get a choice. Falling off a pedestal, whether you choose it or not, can be crippling.

Mom is my hero because she "bucked the call." She refused to move again after our second move because by then I was a teenager and extremely shy, and Mom felt it was important for us to have roots. So, we stayed in the same town and Dad drove to his next call. She may have "bucked the call," but she is one of the most religious people I know. Mom and Dad divorced after twenty-five years of marriage. I can't say that it was solely because of Dad being in ministry, but it sure didn't help. The divorce was a total surprise to everyone but me because they put on a good front to keep up appearances. But where were they to go for help? Our church was against divorce, so it meant Dad had to give up his "calling." Mom stuck it out until we were all out of the house, which was a star in her crown as far as I'm concerned, but it makes me feel guilty to know what she went through for me. Dad was able to find a church after that. The church had relaxed a little in that area.

As a minister's wife, how do you argue when "God is telling me to do this"? Your kids may need you, your marriage may be in ruins and the family unit falling around you, but you need to be somewhere else in the name of God. I realize it must be a difficult decision, and you may think the family will be more likely to forgive you than your congregation. But congregations come and go, and they will be the first to turn on you. And I think God expects you to take care of your family first. I also think that when a person works as a minister 24/7, it is easy to get confused about what God is saying and what is logical and humane. Yes, Mom is my hero.

Embodying Wholistic Transformation: "Arise Woman of God"

I enjoy creative writings. In fact, the story of how Barbara Cooper and I connected involves my sharing original dramatizations of women heroes for an event at the church where Barbara and her husband, Gary, serve. So, when I came across this poem, "Arise Woman of God," by M. S. Lowndes, I knew it must find a place in this book.

Rise up O woman of God
In what He has given you
The things God has laid on your heart
Rise up, go forth, and do

Unlock what God has placed within
The potential you have inside
The world is waiting for your release
To expand your wings and fly

Arise in your God-given gifts
For this is your finest hour
Arise in the Lord's holy might
Ignited and empowered

For God is calling you to come forth
To impact this world for Him
Don't hold back or limit yourself
Let His power arise within

And take His message to the world
To those that have lost their way
For you can surely make a difference
If you'd hear His voice and obey

You shall be strengthened in the Lord
As you begin to arise
Conquering those doubts that pull you down
And believe who you are in Christ

For you shall surely be transformed
As, in you, God increases more
And become a woman of true excellence
Bringing honour to her Lord.
—© M. S. Lowndes

Creating Safety, Support, and Connections: "A SPA Day" Breakthrough

When I first embraced my role as a woman married to a judicatory executive, I started taking a closer look at the entire process of how the denominational system here worked. To my astonishment, I realized that most Women Married to Men in Ministry in our region had never been officially recognized, valued, or thanked for their role and part in the ministry. Nor did there seem to be any system in place for their support and connection. I have since realized this is the rule across America and abroad—not the exception.

I decided to use my position to highlight areas of concern and projects that I found important. The first concern was for Women Married to Men in Ministry, and my solo flight project was called "A SPA Day," an acronym for Spiritual and Physical Awareness.

"The grand experiment," my husband called it. He thought that the women wouldn't like it. After I explained that it was like going to a ball game or meeting on the golf course, he then understood. I was very serious about making sure there was a way that Women Married to Men in Ministry could connect with one another and receive personal support, as well as finding a way to recognize, appreciate, and thank them for their service to the kingdom. Using my experience and expertise as an owner of a paramedical day spa, these women were to be my first-class passengers for a day.

In that effort, I conducted three events for a group of about twenty-five women. We started Spiritual and Physical Awareness Day with a devotional centered around Esther. Then we had some time for personal sharing, and I gave my personal testimony as a way of getting acquainted and establishing a relationship. I had arranged for a massage therapist to be available. We had aromatherapy, lotions and potions, paraffin hand treatments, and hand massages. We also held a fashion show with the Seven-Day Wonder Dress (you wonder how you could wear it for seven days). (Here's the answer—through accessorizing.) We talked about facial shape, hairstyle, eyewear, and cosmetics. We had chocolates and gift baskets and quite an amazingly fine time.

We did all this in order to honor these women and get them connecting with one another. I already knew the "turbulence" each one of them was experiencing in the systemic change operations going on within their churches. But they were not aware that most of them were going through some kind of intense pain and suffering, even though they were all at different stages of the church transformation process. What I hadn't yet realized—because I was new in the position and really a novice—was that many of them didn't know if it was safe to be who they really were. They didn't know if I was a safe person to talk with. Also, they didn't know if they could safely voice anything about the pain that was going on within their church, as it might reflect badly on their husbands.

They did not know me yet, "the boss's wife," and whether I would prove to be safe or a tattletale. Would I go running around, telling my husband or whomever else about their private details? They were very cautious and wondering about what my ulterior motives might be. That's understandable. It takes time for anyone to establish whether you think you can trust another person. This is a process that can only be established through time and relationship. These women had experienced so much betrayal and trust-breaking that, for many of them, establishing trust was a very long process.

We discussed the trust issue in later meetings. One suggestion I made was if you're trying to figure out whether you can trust someone, make up a secret and tell them not to tell anyone else. What you told them won't really matter if they tell, and if they do tell, you know that you cannot trust that person.

As a result of our SPA day and connections that were made there, I invited many of the women to my hotel room the next day. There must have been eighteen to twenty women of all ages in one hotel room—shoes kicked off, sitting cross-legged on the beds, the floor, and the footstools. Everyone was laughing, talking, and being real while getting their hair cut and encouraging one another in the process. It truly was one of the most beautiful experiences that I've ever been a part of, as it provided an opportunity that allowed connection. This event created a good beginning to realizing others had similar experiences and feelings.

PART THREE
Moving toward Mach 10

CHAPTER SIX

VOICES NOW AND THEN

"First Listenings" by Chris Glaser

Whooshing,
Rustling,
Purring,
Silencing,
We're listening;
Speak.

Vibrating,
Echoing,
Exhaling,
Inhaling,
We're listening;
Speak.

Bubbling,
Fizzing,
Slamming,
Popping,
We're listening;
Speak.[1]

What's in a Voice?

I began to think about the sound barrier and the implications of the word *sound*, not just the violent shaking of breaking the sound barrier but also finding our voice in it. I decided to do a search of the word *voice*. I wasn't sure exactly what I would find, but it turned out to be a fascinating, diverse topic. Mostly what I discovered was about advocacy groups. I discovered a lot about the science of voice. But the concept is also applied to such diverse areas as social justice (animal rights, equal rights, political action groups), art (color design, galleries), and technology (VoIP—Voice over Internet Protocol, voice-over talent used for commercial purposes, and voice recognition programs, which I use for typing and e-mails . . . and find a mixed blessing).

So many different definitions and uses for this word! And yet, with all this diversity, it seems that what it really boils down to is that when *voice* is used, it stands for something far bigger than just a series of sound waves. Voice stands for service to humankind. God blessed and blesses us with a spiritual voice to communicate with him, even if we are physically mute. The human voice also has a powerful ability to impact those around us.

According to renowned sound researcher Don Campbell, surprisingly, the human voice is one of the most powerful healing tools we possess—a tool we carry with us wherever we go.[2] Our bodies love the sound of our own voice. It creates the perfect vibration that not only matches our physical body (resonates) but also honestly describes the present state of our emotional body. In our voice, there are reflections of our day. All of the tensions, joys, relaxations, and frustrations are imprinted here. Everything is reflected in the voice honestly. Every time we hear the "tone" of our spouse's voice, it indicates mood. That explains why our voices are never exactly the same. Sounds produced by us reverberate through the body and are able to remove tension and pain. It may be when we groan, sigh, cry, moan, laugh, or just say *ahh*, *ohhh*, or *ouch*.

The vibrations of our voice offer a sort of inner massage—healing from the inside out—perhaps most especially laughter. Maybe that is why the book of Proverbs tells us that "a cheerful heart is a good medicine" (Proverbs 17:22). More technically, I found that our voice's vibration creates a notable effect on two of our most sensitive physiological systems: the neurological and the endocrine systems. For instance, the sounds we make strongly vibrate the brain, the pituitary and hypothalamus in particular. Even Western medicine has found that the vibration of the voice has a positive effect on blood pressure, heart rate, and pain relief. With our voice, God has given us a wonderful tool that we need in order to have whole and healthy lives.

But what happens when our voice is silenced, either physically or metaphorically?

Women from Before Help Us Find Our Voice Today

When my daughter was a little girl, I did not want to read her some of the fairy tales that often portrayed femininity as a passive concept. Such as Cinderella, who was miserable until her fairy godmother appeared and she met the handsome prince. Or, Sleeping Beauty, who was "unconscious" until kissed by the handsome prince.

I prefer looking at the way the Bible describes women. These women are strong, powerful, capable, and intelligent. These women were bold risk-takers. These women were women who dared. For many years, I have presented narrative dramatizations of biblical women. They have been my mentors, and it is exciting to bring their voices alive today as beacons of hope to what we might attain.

Abigail leads the way for us in finding our voices today. I'm well acquainted with her because on many occasions my husband and I perform this part of Scripture as David and Abigail in dramatic presentations. I find Abigail particularly courageous, given the time that she lived.

According to 1 Samuel 25, Abigail is the wife of a very wealthy man, Nabal, whose name means "fool." Nabal owns a huge ranch. It is festival time, a time of sheep counting and shearing, and Nabal is throwing a grand party.

Meanwhile, David and his men are living in the wilderness after the death of Samuel. They take it upon themselves to protect the herds of local ranchers from attacks by wild animals and from marauders. David sends his men with a message to Nabal to claim a portion of their compensation. But Nabal spurns the request and insults David publicly instead: "Who is this David . . . son of Jesse? Tell him to go back to his master where he belongs. Why should I take my hard-earned spoils of labor and give it to these men coming from who knows where?" This is an outrage. It infuriates David. Now he is out to seek revenge and plans to kill Nabal and his entire household.

Abigail must have had a reputation for wisdom and justice because Nabal's head shepherd Hezron comes to her and tells her what has happened. She listens. It's as though he approaches her with an expectation that she will intervene in this volatile situation. Abigail's mind must have been going a hundred miles an hour just to keep pace with the pounding of her heart. Quickly, she takes action. She loads up her donkeys with wine, roasted grain, raisins, and cakes of figs. Then she and her servants ride out with trepidation to meet David.

Would he even receive her? Would he have her killed before she could even approach? If she could say anything to him, how could she persuade David to change his intent?

As Abigail approaches David and his band, she quickly gets off her donkey and bows low before David. She speaks: "The LORD has kept you, my master, from bloodshed and from avenging yourself with your own hands, as surely as the LORD lives and as you live, may your enemies and all who intend to harm my master be like Nabal. [A fool.] And let this gift, which your servant has brought to my master, be given to the men who follow you. Please forgive your servant's offense, for the LORD will certainly make a lasting dynasty for my master, because he fights the LORD's battles. Let no wrongdoing be found in you as long as you live. Even though someone is pursuing you to take your life, the life of my master will be bound securely. . . . But the lives of your enemies, [God] will hurl away as from the pocket of a sling. When the LORD has done for my master every good thing he promised concerning him and has appointed him leader over Israel, my master will not have on his conscience the staggering burden of needless bloodshed or of having avenged himself. And when the LORD has brought my master success, remember your servant" (1 Samuel 25:26-31 NIV).

Can you imagine the tension in the air as she waits? It must have felt like an eternity passing, awaiting his response.

David is stunned by this woman and her actions. Finally, David speaks to Abigail: "Praise be to the LORD, the God of Israel, who has sent you today to meet me. May you be blessed for your good judgment and for keeping me from bloodshed this day and from avenging myself with my own hands. Otherwise, as surely as the LORD, the God of Israel, lives, who has kept me from harming you, if you had not come quickly to meet me, not one . . . belonging to Nabal would have been left alive by daybreak" (1 Samuel 25:32-34 NIV).

Abigail took decisive action and modeled bravery that honored God and saved her entire household. The Scripture doesn't tell us if she was afraid or not. (If it had been me, I'm sure I would have been much afraid!) And she gave voice to reason, truth, and justice. Abigail did not appeal to David from some sense of personal obligation but to his higher self and God's higher calling. She did not manipulate him emotionally but spoke to him in a clear and bold voice, reminding him of his greater purpose, vision, and mission.

The risks were great for her in giving voice and taking action. Not only was she defying her husband, she was doing it in a very public manner! Abigail had likely suffered Nabal's wrath for much less than this. She did not know if she would die at the hand of David or his men, or at the hand of Nabal, but she went because she knew it was the right thing to do, the only thing she could do. By the way, Abigail accepts the marriage proposal of David after the death of her husband and becomes one of his wives.

Who might be delivered from danger by our careful listening and courageous action? By our humbling ourselves to do the right thing? By being afraid but doing it anyway? By our bold voice-giving to righteousness and justice?

Instigating Systemic Change

For well over three millennia, women have been living in inflexible rigid systems designed to keep them grounded in subservient roles without ever hoping to be able to soar, and yet, soar they have!

Look at Tamar, Rahab, Abigail, Esther, Deborah, Ruth, Mary mother of Christ, Mary and Martha, Lydia, Priscilla, Puah and Shiphrah—the midwives, the Syro-Phoenician woman, the woman at the well, and Mary Magdalene.

Every single one of these women was a (super)natural barrier breaker.

The fuel they used to break through social and spiritual barriers was a cause above and beyond themselves. These women of Scripture have left us a legacy of flying, without ever dreaming of a heavier-than-air machine taking to the sky. They took the weight of their position in life and launched it—for a greater purpose beyond themselves. As a consequence, they changed the course of their own life, the lot of womankind, and the history of humanity. Without knowing it, they left us a navigation tool kit—a flight operation manual. Theirs was a flight from oppression to freedom while claiming their airspace on earth.

The Strength of Five Sisters

The Hebrew Scriptures share the story of the daughters of Zelophehad (Numbers 27:1-10), five sisters who lived during the exodus of the Israelites from Egypt. These five women didn't know about air travel—but they knew about the flight of an eagle, and on the day that they made a collective decision to voice their petition to God, that was the day that they took flight.

Their father, Zelophehad, came from the tribe of Manasseh. His daughters' names were Noah, Hoglah, Milcah, Mahlah, and Tirzah. Zelophehad died during the forty years when the Israelites were wandering around in the wilderness. As he had no sons, that meant no male heirs. Each tribe would have an allotment in the promised land of Israel—but it would be apportioned to male householders only. So, this was a critical concern for a family that now consisted only of women. These five sisters raised the issue of women's rights and obligations to inherit property in the absence of a male heir in the family.

Zelophehad's daughters were wise, seeing that they were equal in merit. So they voiced their case to Moses, Eleazar the priest, the chieftains, and the whole assembly. These five women stood before all of them. They noted that their father was not one of Korah's followers (Numbers 27:3). Zelophehad's daughters stated that if they were not to inherit land, his name would be lost to his clan.

Can you just imagine the interchange these five sisters must have had before they were able to take such a courageous step? After all, if we take meanings of their Hebrew names as indicators, this was a very diverse group: Noah ("to rest" or "to comfort"), Hoglah ("bold one" or "to uphold"), Milcah ("queen" or "counselor"), Mahlah ("sickly one"), and Tirzah ("pleasant" or "favorable one"). When I perform dramatic presentations of these women, I give each a persona based on her name and its meaning: Hoglah has a strong, bold, forceful voice. Tirzah is very traditional and pleasant. Milcah acts as a wise counselor with queenly formability. Mahlah is weak, unsure, and hesitant; she needs convincing. Noah is a peacemaker and wants everyone to be comfortable in the status quo.

I'm sure it was a lively discussion, with many different perspectives but with the same common mission to accomplish. They demonstrated wisdom in how they raised their case, giving voice to their cause for justice. They had just cause, but they were certainly going against traditions since at that time in history a woman herself was counted as a piece of property.

Upon hearing them, Moses took their case directly to God. God spoke, telling Moses that the plea of Zelophehad's daughters was just, and that they should be granted their father's inheritance, which was the holding of his land. Later, Gilead, the family head of the clan of Manasseh, also appealed to Moses, Eleazer the priest, and the chieftains. He argued that if Zelophehad's daughters married into another Israelite tribe, their share would be lost to the tribe of Manasseh and added to the portion of the tribe into which they married. Moses, at God's bidding, instructed the Israelites that the plea of the tribal leaders was just, and that Zelophehad's daughters were free to marry anyone they wished but only among the men of the tribe of Manasseh. Zelophehad's daughters did as God had commanded Moses, and each married within the tribe of Manasseh.

After the death of Moses when the Israelites entered the land, Zelophehad's daughters appeared once again before Eleazer the priest, Joshua, and the chieftains. They reminded them that God had commanded Moses to grant them their inheritance among their kinsmen, and these five women received a portion in the holdings of Manasseh's side of the Jordan River (Joshua 17:3-6). They persisted in advocating for their portion, even after God's declaration had been given. They showed amazing courage, and they shared the strength of a collective voice—a voice of reason and justice. God heard their petition and affirmed their right of ownership as women. This tradition is still part of our legacy today, established so long ago by these five women—sisters—daughters of Zelophehad.

These brave women model for us a well-thought-out plan, done in a timely fashion, and presented with good reason. As women involved in church system transformations, we, too, can create solid plans, for instance, in regard to how we see our position or role as women in ministry or Women Married to Men in Ministry. It will be necessary to prepare well and communicate that plan wisely, whether in spoken or written form, to the leadership and congregants of the church and judicatory.

We need to give ourselves permission to voice our own needs and desires. This is not just critical for us, but it will begin to create new paradigms and structures for those who will follow—a legacy and inheritance of even greater freedom to speak forth truth.

Barbara's Story of Learning NOT to Speak

Scripture says that our words have the power to bless or curse, that our tongue starts wildfires or, conversely, it tames and soothes. In Old Testament times, blessings by fathers upon their children (or lack of blessings) affected the family's future. By our voice—our words—we contribute to one another and, ultimately, to the world.

My collaborating author, Barbara, has many thoughts about the subject of voice and words, about "what" we say to self and others, and the words that we hear, filter, take in, or reject. She says that, for good or ill, words voiced aloud impact the health, happiness, and wholeness of ourselves and those around us.

Many of God's creatures vocalize but not all have words. As Barbara found out early in life, sometimes we have neither. In writing this book, she was reminded of a traumatizing incident early in her own life that altered her willingness to voice and even blocked some uses of vocalizing.

"Early one morning," Barbara says, "I was sitting in a spot of sunshine, waking up, and thinking about the issue of 'voice.' Alone in the room, I began to practice intonation—humming out loud. I noticed the resonation throughout my skull and throat. It made me think about what a silent person I am, and how unusual—almost uncomfortable—it is to hear myself vocalize.

"Suddenly, I flashed back to my knowledge of the very early beginnings of my life. As vulnerable babies, my sister Rita and I were abandoned in an apartment. Rita was just three-and-a-half at the time, and I was barely ten weeks old. Through a number of very sad circumstances, we were left there alone for two full weeks. I was near death when we were found.

"Of course, I have no direct memories of this, but Rita has told me her haunting recollections. She said I cried incessantly at first. Rita knew I was hungry, so she fed me all the milk that was in the refrigerator. Then she tried to get me to eat crackers, until she finished them up herself when I wouldn't eat them. Then she tried to feed me tomatoes, as there was a bushel basket of them underneath the table—which was where she sat for much of the ordeal. And still, I cried and cried. Then, finally, I stopped.

"I learned as an infant that vocalization—crying—didn't bring help. It wasn't heard. No, I wasn't heard! I think I learned then to stop crying throughout my life, unless in secret/private, in order to save my strength."

How hard it is to "unlearn *not* to speak," yet how necessary! In an account Barbara wrote of the impact of this incident, she goes on to reflect that each of us thinks and speaks words of blessing and cursing to ourselves. Sometimes our "self-talk" is actually vocalized, other times not. As we think of Women Married to Men in Ministry, how important it is to know our own voice and God's voice, to set boundaries around the messages we accept or reject. Words are so important in the area of identity. By them we receive answers to the same question Jesus asked, "Who do you *say* that I am?"

Thus, for myself and so many others, Barbara believes the following poem by Marge Piercy, "Unlearning to not speak," expresses our fe-male reality. However, she also thinks similar feelings extend to all who experience marginalization in their humanity: "Finding and then expressing our voice will indeed begin to break the sound barrier," she states. "Silent, grunting, groaning, shrieking, vocalizing—then communicating—and, ultimately speaking the truth in love. Transformation begins within; it is personal first, then, dare I say, we can deal with the political and institutional. When using our voice, we find the truth that 'perfect love casts out fear.' But we must first learn, or relearn, to speak."

> Blizzards of paper
> in slow motion
> sift through her.
> In nightmares she suddenly recalls
> a class she signed up for
> but forgot to attend.
> Now it is too late.
> Now it is time for finals:
> losers will be shot.
> Phrases of men who lectured her
> drift and rustle in piles:
> Why don't you speak up?
> Why are you shouting?
> You have the wrong answer,
> wrong line, wrong face.
> They tell her she is womb-man,

babymachine, mirror image, toy,
earth mother and penis-poor,
a dish of synthetic strawberry icecream
She grunts to a halt.
She must learn again to speak
starting with *I*
starting with *We*
starting as the infant does
with her own true hunger
and pleasure
and rage.[3]

CHAPTER SEVEN

Co-ministry Couples and Copiloting the Plane

So What's "The Right Stuff"?

Even though there were thirteen women being trained as astronauts in the early 1960s, it's generally seen that men are the only ones with "The Right Stuff." The movie adaptation of Tom Wolfe's novel by that title shows the bravery and the bravado of the seven men who were first to fly into outer space. In 2003, a twentieth-anniversary special edition of the film was released. In the DVD documentaries, Tom Wolfe said that he found the same theme emerging, both from and about the early transonic test pilots and astronauts. "The right stuff," he states, "is the willingness to risk death on a daily basis."

As women involved in radical systemic change in churches, there is no doubt that we, too, have "the right stuff." We prove it by paying the price of death to self daily. That is a legitimate cost to our call for obedient service as disciples of Jesus Christ. But, there are some prices we pay that are illegitimate—and ultimately poisonous to ourselves, our marriage, and our family. So, we need to consider how to insulate ourselves from exposure to unnecessary depletion or "death."

In writing this book, I often found myself struggling spiritually and emotionally. I do not want to talk about feminism, nor do I want to talk about submission. I want to talk about something in the middle with no name at the present time. It's hard to describe. It's not about a mushy middle or fence-sitting but about women being decisive. It's not about women being anemic or pathetic but about women being vital. The best that I can come up with is that **God created Fe-male-ness.**

This entity, Fe-male, God believed was crucial to his creation and Adam's effectiveness in fulfilling his role. So he created them male and fe-male (a part of and yet set apart from). And maybe "the real stuff" is our Fe-male-ness counterpart expression to "the right stuff" that has typically been applied only to men. It's about God's creation and gifting of fe-males, not about the fe-male interactions with the male.

In finding this Fe-male-ness, once again I'm drawn back to the lives of the women in the Scripture whom I consider my mentors. Their voices always stay in my mind's ear. With only one or two exceptions, they did not work within the established system at all. Instead, they worked outside the system or alongside it. So, while it may sound like I'm asking women to "blow up the system," what I really want to do is issue a call to action—not suggest a passive or aggressive response to the system or even a dropping out.

In this, we should note that *faulty church culture systems do not work for anyone*—not just women. We also want to be sure that our identity is being propelled through the voice of God, or by the voice of God in our voice-finding. For we who are women in ministry and Women Married to Men in Ministry, that is part of "the right stuff," too, and "the real stuff" as well.

Living in the Shadows, or Walking in the Light

For some Women Married to Men in Ministry, marriage does not provide the protection and nurture needed to sustain a healthy personal identity and a healthy family. Here are some of the specific concerns voiced by women who live in the shadows.

A woman e-mailed this to me: "I'm afraid I don't have relationships with any of the wives of men in ministry. I don't fit in very well with many of them. Would be glad to converse with you about anything you like. I could sure use a pen pal. . . . [My husband] left yesterday for an out-of-state meeting and will be back tomorrow. He has been away from home most of the month. Will be glad to have him back. Heaven knows even though I was with him at the meeting where you and I met, he was not with me, if you know what I mean."

I asked another woman in ministry whose husband is also in ministry to share what she sees as the single worst problem in the "pastor's wife" stereotype. She said, "I am going to guess here and say that it is playing second fiddle to the church."

One key way to progress toward healthiness in marriage, family, and ministry is to bring our co-ministry styles into the open so we can take a look at them. Only then can we be more intentional in optimizing the opportunities God has providentially placed before us.

The realities of ministry are like the rules of "community property": what belongs to one spouse belongs to both. Like it or not, Women Married to Men in Ministry share the activities and impacts of ministry's labors, stresses, and joys. A couple in ministry needs to think of themselves at least as co-ministers, if not copilots. In my thinking, *this is non-negotiable*. Without a co-ministry strategy as a mutual understanding—or as a covenant, even—it is impossible to shelter our marriage and ensure it stays healthy. (In the pressure cooker of turnaround churches and systemic changes, agreement on the approach is especially important!)

Both the husband and wife must be in complete **agreement** and not allow anyone to drive a wedge between them, either by words or behaviors or a crazy, unhealthy schedule of activities. Healthy boundaries include: (1) what we believe and (2) how we function as co-ministers.

On the first issue, I would suggest that we develop agreement in six different belief areas that directly affect a healthy marriage and a healthy church. Some are universal, and others will depend more on our ministry context.

1. Who we are as a couple—our marriage is a top priority, even above the congregation and judicatory. We can only lead people to the heights of healthiness and growth we ourselves develop.

2. Our Mission—to become a whole and healthy body of believers who take the Great Commission seriously and are outwardly focused.

3. Our Vision—a changed community, with new Christ followers being developed by our discipleship as we ourselves continue to change and grow.

4. Our Values—[identify three to five key values that guide us in carrying out our mission and vision.]

5. Our Strategy—[identify the roles of paid staff, volunteer leaders, congregational ministries, and so on.]

6. *Our Organization*—[identify who the leaders are: minister, co-minister, board, and so on.]

On the second issue, I have observed three different ways that couples go about fulfilling their functional roles of co-ministers. There may be other approaches that emerge, but these give some basic options for us to consider.

Option 1—Coequals. In this view, both spouses view their roles as essentially the same. They are equals but divide the labor in relation to gifts, abilities, and talents. This approach will probably require each spouse to preach with equal frequency, as leadership in turnaround churches is often viewed as those exercising "up-front ministry."

Option 2—First among Equals. Here, one spouse functions like an Executive Minister to the other, who is the Senior Minister/Pastor. Sharing of the preaching role is not as crucial in this model as in the "equal partners with same responsibilities" approach.

Option 3—Equal Importance, Different Realms. In this approach, one spouse oversees those aspects of the church directly related to its growth and health (for example, teaching, equipping, leading). The other spouse leads in areas not directly related to the growth of the church but still contributes to its health. In this model, the preaching role is less likely to be shared.

Regardless of which co-ministry option is our preference and practice, some leadership issues simply require both spouses to work together. For instance, church leaders need to conduct "mini-interventions" each and every week. (Here, I'm using the term *intervention* as similar to a stock-market correction or an in-flight course correction.) If these interventions are not carried out regularly, there is institutional drift that moves issues away from the mission, vision, and values of the organization. Generally, the partner who is better at conducting a particular kind of intervention needs to take that responsibility. However, the more comfortable each is with the entire process, the more they need to conduct course corrections together, even though one may take the lead.

Mind the Gap!

The realities of partnership between men and women in ministry, and healthy ministerial marriages, are simply "off the radar" within some congregations of many denominations and among their leaders. Sharing this book offers a natural opportunity to broach this subject in formal and informal settings of leaders and spouses. However, too many times the immediate response is to change the subject. It's as if a "successful" ministry and a "successful" pastoral marriage have absolutely no relationship to each other. The inability of people to make the connection between the two just astounds me! Ironically, perhaps that in itself is some of the strongest evidence that this book is needed.

At one particular judicatory meeting, I received such incredulous responses to the idea of networking sessions for women in ministry and Women Married to Men in Ministry that it got me thinking about how we need to "mind the gap," lest we collapse into a black hole. How is it that in 2007, the gap could be so great between welcoming women into discussions that will impact their lives so directly? That question took me to a *Science Daily* article on the uncovering of causes for the huge gap in the Van Allen Belts. (Don't get too hung up in the technical details; the analogy is relevant.) I wanted to see what lessons God had embedded in the universe about the gap.

> Radio waves in space, known as plasmaspheric hiss, are responsible for the formation of the slot region between the inner and outer radiation belt. While the details of the loss process are well known, the source of these waves has been a matter of intense debate for several decades. There are two competing theories. One theory maintains that the radio waves are generated locally via natural turbulence in space, arising from particles injected during enhanced magnetic activity driven by the Sun. The other theory suggests that the radio waves, generated by lightning activity on Earth, leak into space and evolve into hiss after multiple reflections in space.
>
> Enhanced fluxes of energetic particles damage spacecraft and are a risk to humans in space. Improved understanding of the weather in space will help protect the satellites and astronauts operating in these regions.[1]

I consider the plasmaspheric hiss to be like the static nature of discussions of whether Women Married to Men in Ministry should be included in relevant conversations regarding ministries of which they are a part. As agents of change, we need to be monitoring weather in our space on a regular basis, as there are so many different forms of turbulence. Also, competing voices injected into our everyday reality not only cause the hiss but also cause the gap to grow wider, which damages us in the process. Women must not be taken for granted, but considered in the equation.

An amazing amount of evidence about the gap between healthy marriage and healthy ministry appeared during the writing of this book. In April 2007, Mary Winkler was convicted of voluntary manslaughter in the March 2006 shooting death of her pastor husband. Meanwhile, magazines and journals, websites, and blogs all brought forth research and opinions on issues concerning the pressures of living as a pastor's wife. A story in *Time* magazine was especially poignant:

> Though often educated and deeply thoughtful, many PWs [Pastors' Wives] say they can't partake in theological debates at church lest their opinions be interpreted as their husbands'. There, too, the Internet provides an outlet. Lora Horn, 35, a mother of two from Las Vegas, moved to rural Garrett, Ind., in 2004. "I never fit into the mold," says the former social worker. "I was a tomboy. I'm not domestic. I'm intellectual. I'm an introvert. I'm a person who likes to buck the norm." She began blogging a year ago as RebelliousPastorsWife to "have the conversations I wasn't having in real life"—about "theology, politics, family life, knitting, baseball." Recently she struck up a heated conversation online about the role of the sacraments, a subject she would never bring up at Bible study. She has learned that any pronouncement by a pastor's family is fraught. During a tense discussion about renting the church to another congregation, their son asked where Sunday school would be held, leading churchgoers to think the pastor was against the plan (he wasn't). It's hard to separate her husband's identity from hers, says Horn. "Our teachings are clear, that it's the pastor who's called, not the wife. But in reality . . ." she sighs.[2]

The Quest: Why This Journey

Though there are intense pressures and difficulties facing ministerial families, that does not mean all couples are falling into the gap. There are still visionary couples who are adventurers and explorers of the faith, in spite of all the plasmaspheric hiss. There are couples willing to go above and beyond to meet God and his word. They imagine they could be a part of changing this world forever. A mission guides their lives. They function under the control of one commander, Jesus Christ.

The Scripture gives us an example of a ministry couple in Priscilla and Aquila. Priscilla seems to be every bit as dynamic as her husband as they functioned as a pastoral team. They conducted home churches both in Rome and in Corinth. According to Acts 18:26, both Priscilla and Aquila had a teaching ministry and taught Apollos spiritual truths. Like Aquila, she shared the task of fellow workers in the area of her giftedness. We are aware that some women do not want to be a part of an up-front ministry. These women need to be able to define their role and position to suit their personal identity and gifting. But there are some Women Married to Men in Ministry who, as one minister put it, only "like to lead in silent prayer." We were all created differently, but all meant to be conformed to the image of Christ, nothing more or nothing less.

> "God authorized and commanded me to commission you: Go out and train everyone you meet, far and near, in this way of life, marking them by baptism in the threefold name: Father, Son, and Holy Spirit. Then instruct them in the practice of all I have commanded you. I'll be with you as you do this, day after day after day, right up to the end of the age." (Matthew 28:18-20 *The Message*)

These visionary couples dare to believe this Scripture is true. They hear the call and go forward. Then they face the "Now what?" question. They know the "mother ship," the church, needs a radical retrofit. It cannot be church as usual anymore. Here we are at a hinge point in history. In many ways, our society reflects the time of the first-century church with the addition of technology and thousands of years of advancement in science, medicine, engineering, space exploration, and so on. Yet church growth in First World countries lags, which presents us with the questions of *Where do we go from here?* and *How do we get there?*

Some contemporary couples in ministry show similar vision for partnering or copiloting in ministry. For instance, the little church that began at a drive-in theater and eventually became The Crystal Cathedral was founded in the 1950s by Robert and Arvella Schuller, working side by side. Their son, Robert Anthony, and his wife, Donna, took on that same mantle of partnership as he was installed in January 2006 as the new Senior Pastor at The Crystal Cathedral. An April 2007 article in *Church Executive* magazine notes that, as a first-ever practice in the Reformed Church in America, Donna participated in the installation liturgy, agreeing publicly that she "accepted the role and responsibility as Robert's wife to lead this church into the future."

It also states that "Donna Schuller works with her husband in ministry at the church, travels frequently with him and serves on the church's leadership team. She took a group of women to Shreveport [Louisiana], last year to rebuild a home after Hurricane Katrina, is engaged with a homeless shelter for women and children called Isaiah House in Santa Ana [California], and has a heart for the modern-day sexual slavery issues coming recently to public attention."[3]

The Holy Spirit is hovering over the church at this time—a providential timing for us both to identify the gap and forge new ways of closing the gap as ministry couples emerge as role models. *What might then come next!*

Gary's and Barbara's Stories of Copiloting through Transformation

My coauthor, Barbara, and her husband, Gary, have themselves gone through the breaking-the-sound-barrier process in a turnaround church in our region. Their stories of personal transformation in the midst of that systemic church change also demonstrate a great role-modeling of what it means for a ministry couple to copilot in this process.

Gary's Story: Pilot's Log—Stardate 2007: "Houston, We Have a Problem"

How often on this transformational journey, now into its seventh year, have I come before the Lord—overwhelmed and seemingly unprepared for the task.

Transformation—the word is exciting and sounds faintly biblical. After all, are we not to be transformed through the renewing of our mind? In truth, no one has prepared this turnaround-church pilot for that change-and-transition task. Seminaries still teach their pilots to fly a stable, DC-3—slow and steady. "Don't worry about the turbulence," they tell you. "It'll pass." In truth, had it not been for my years of business and parenting—and a great copilot in Barbara—I would have crashed and burned some time ago.

It turns out that everyone wants to fly at the speed of sound and beyond, soar to the very boundaries of space, everyone wants to pilot a church into mega status. But what about the strain that g-forces exert on your body? What about the other potential dangers? No, they don't teach you that in seminary—because few if any of the faculty have stretched the boundaries of transformation themselves.

Congregations tell you that they want to undergo transformation for the Great Commission—but then again, the elders of Israel told Moses that they wanted to leave the slavery of Egypt and follow him to God's promised land. Now, as then, people are not ready to let go of the comfort of the known and embrace the dangers and discomforts of the unknown.

Our once great, century-old congregation struggled with the realities of its situation. For them, *Houston, we have a problem*, meant that they had the wrong pastor to carry them back to the glory days of the past. After dumping one pilot and waiting on the tarmac with three interim pastors, the desperate congregation found us. A brief preflight check by consultants uncovered a number of serious flaws, but the report was shelved—never shared with me as the new pilot. Its pride and traditions kept it in a perpetual state of denial. As the rest of the surrounding community flew by on faster F18s or comfortable 757s, people in our church faithfully boarded their DC-3 every week and waited for the new pilot to get them to their destination.

Most of our traditional churches—this one being no different—are in a state of emergency. Hemorrhaging members, overwhelmed with the challenges of their community, are ill-prepared to take decisive action. *Houston, we have an emergency* means just that—a serious problem that must be addressed quickly, efficiently, and effectively—or the spacecraft and its crew are lost. Decaying orbit and loss of cabin pressure and life-sustaining oxygen mean that the pilot may only have one chance at the proper attitude of transformation.

The stress is imperceptible at first: fatigue, sleeplessness, irritability. These and my rising blood pressure were only a few of the symptoms that began to affect my judgment and my relationship with my copilot, my wife, Barbara. Had I not had such a caring and committed spouse for this journey, I probably would have chosen a safer place to pilot. I can only imagine what a pastor with a struggling marriage and family could be going through. If an astronaut candidate with those problems asked me my opinion, I'd tell him to stick to flying DC-3s! Plus, be prepared for sudden loss of cabin pressure, drop in altitude, and lots of pain. You will not enter transformation of a church without yourself becoming transformed in the process—it will be up to you if it is a crash-and-burn or a happy landing.

Competitive by nature, I have had to contend with repeated "ego adjustments." (I suspect the Holy Spirit is as much about my transformation as that of the church.) While I know and seek to employ all the techniques that church growth experts propose, in general these don't translate well to the mean streets of our community. *Houston, we tried that, but nothing's happening.* Frustration and fear of failure are my companions. *What if I break the church?* a quiet inner voice nags. On more than one occasion, I have found myself like Scottie, the Star Trek flight engineer, telling the Lord, "Cap'n, I'm giv'n' it all she's got!"

On more than one occasion, I have written a letter I didn't send, checked my mouth before the wrong words slipped out, and asked God for some good old-fashioned Old Testament justice—upon my detractors, that is. But I have never forgotten the mission. In the midst of the most difficult times, loss in attendance, declining giving, frayed nerves—I have remembered God's words: "Stand firm." It hurts to lose a crew member. It hurts to lose a church member, often one who has attended longer than I have been a Christian. It hurts to lose contributors.

But the mission of transformation comes first. Experts contend that less than 14 percent of the San Francisco Bay Area population attends religious services on a regular basis—this includes all religions. My best guess is that it is probably closer to 4 percent. If that is to change into kingdom growth, our region needs more healthy churches that truly carry out the Great Commission.

Transformation is a misunderstood concept, though. For "the churched," it means redecorating the sanctuary and refilling the empty pews with the same folks who already used the "escape capsule" of going to another area church that "has it together" or moving to the suburbs to escape the city. Our assignment was to transition from traditional to missional, an unpopular one with the churched set, it turns out.

In February 2001, I stood before this congregation. They were enthusiastic and hopeful. I was filled with excitement and energy for the flight. "Our mission," I stated, "is to reach the lost, the least, and the lonely of our area with the love of Christ." In the seats that day was a visitor, a practicing Zen-Buddhist who, it turns out, became our first convert of the transformation. Since then, Sikhs and Muslims, agnostics and atheists, broken people and blessed people, felons set free and Nepalese refugees—needy people of many types have joined our flight crew and the kingdom.

The transformation is happening before my eyes, but the personal cost has been high.

Frankly, I presumed that by now we would have "been there," that we would have arrived. I'd have written the book, conducted the seminars, and made the consulting rounds. Instead, like Moses, I'm to take the spacecraft on one more orbit as the transformation continues.

I've learned a lot about myself and the people of our church by rereading the wilderness journey of Moses and the Israelites. It may not be a story of flight, but it is surely one of fortitude—and future. Like Moses, I now know that I will not see the completion of the mission. I have lost over half the crew I started with, lost my original leadership team, and had to contend with the not-so-quiet rancor and resentment of those who called me here on this mission. Nonetheless, a new crew is coming on board. We have repaired the ailing craft and plugged in the mission coordinates, and with the right leadership, this church will fly faithfully into the future God intended.

As I was writing this today, I looked at a picture of Sunesia. A Thai immigrant, she recently renounced her lifelong Buddhist faith and accepted Jesus Christ as her Lord and Savior. She was baptized on Easter. The photographer captured her utter joy, with one arm thrust heavenward and jubilation on her face. Just maybe, that is *Houston, mission accomplished.*

Barbara's Story:
Flight Attendant or Copilot?

"Please finish stowing all carry-ons in the overhead bins or underneath the seat in front of you. The captain has turned on the seat belt light. Please fasten your seat belts securely for takeoff. Flight attendants, please return to your seat for takeoff."

Flight attendant or copilot? Two very different ranks with very different job descriptions, not to mention very different compensations. Both positions are necessary to ensure a safe and comfortable flight. One, however, resides in the seat next to the pilot and assists in flying the plane. The other walks to and fro in the cabin, providing the passengers comfort by answering call lights, serving beverages, distributing blankets and pillows.

Invited by the pastor's search committee to speak at one of my husband's final interview meetings, I addressed a specific question fielded directly to me: "If Gary becomes our pastor, what do you see as your role in the church?" Excitedly naive and thinking my answer would be understood, I responded, "God has called us as a co-ministering couple, so we'll minister in the church together." It turns out that my view of co-ministry was not immediately understood. The church's definition fit more with the pastor's-wife-as-flight-attendant model—mine was as the pastor's copilot.

I first assumed the position of Woman Married to a Man in Ministry during the time my husband was fulfilling his "supervised ministry internship" at seminary. We had entered seminary together, both expecting our divinity degrees to launch us into pastoral ministry. During Gary's internship as pastoral interim at a small and dying church in the northern California wine country, I soon came to learn in this conservative congregation that, at best, I might some day be considered for a place on the deacon's committee but that a woman in pastoral leadership was impossible. Although stunned, deflated, and briefly depressed at this pronouncement upon my future, I shook it off and began to serve anyway. (After all, the biblical definition of the word *minister* is indeed *servant*.)

Rewind back to the pastoral search committee interview—my copiloting response was received with smiles and nodding. We signed on—my husband as pastor and me as the woman married to him as "pastor's wife." Hearing God's call to ministry had no relationship to my being the spouse of a minister—it meant I also was called as a minister. Thus began a long journey of finding my place, and, more important, my identity in this place we were called to.

Personal transformation does not take place in a vacuum. Still in progress, my transformation has largely been through the process of surrendering repeatedly to the flight attendant role. My dreams of ministry faded day by day. They became lost in a maze of wall painting, closet cleaning, cookie baking, paper folding, meal making, smiling, and waving.

After seven years in this fuselage of transformation, opportunities for increased spiritual leadership in the church have slowly emerged. To the credit of our church elder board, they have begun to recognize my giftings. They officially licensed me for ministry and are proceeding with the process of my ordination. Although this provides me with the copiloting platform, it is yet to be seen how this will all translate into actual ministry as copilot to my piloting pastor husband.

In our denomination we have found few successful role models of pastors and their wives who serve side by side in spiritual ministry within the same congregation. In the reality of the turnaround, transformational church experience, the mentoring outlook is even more bleak. I can't honestly say that we have found even one couple who serve together in vocational ministry in the same church with both as professional, ordained staff, where both husband and wife are effectively employed as co-ministering spiritual leaders. I believe there are many reasons for this—not the least of which is long-standing church culture and doctrinal positions that limit the role of women in the church.

I feel blessed to have a pastor-spouse with a natural egalitarian nature; he celebrates the spiritual giftedness of women and men and seeks to encourage the development and use of everyone's gifts within the body of Christ. However, as Senior Pastor-Pilot, his first concern is for the passengers in the cabin and those waiting to board the plane. Therefore the tasks and duties of his copilot (me) include whatever needs to be done. This often translates to my taking on the role of flight attendant for those waiting to be served.

My belief of God's calling in my life stands strongly against the turbulence and winds of opposition to my progress. In moments of weakness, I question God: *Did I misunderstand you, Lord? Perhaps we weren't called to copilot this plane.* Then, an opportunity for Gary and me to work together in a significant spiritual endeavor occurs, and God orchestrates wonderful results—salvific kingdom results. It's those moments that keep me flying. God has given me the wings, and I must rely on him to provide the opportunities to fly.

CHAPTER EIGHT

TRANSFORMED THROUGH THE JOURNEY

Out-of-This-World Transformations: Eileen Collins, Astronaut

I recently watched a C-Span program where Women in Leadership awards were presented by former president George Bush and Barbara Bush. Their four guests were Harriet Miers, Chris Evert, Eileen Collins, and Teri Hatcher.

I found Eileen Collins's comments about NASA most interesting. First of all, she said that her faith played an enormous role in her profession—she could not imagine anyone strapping themselves to a rocket unless they had faith! Can anyone out there relate?

Then she talked about the effects that being in outer space had on the body, things that I had not heard spoken of before. Colonel Collins stated that astronauts must drink a lot of water to counteract the high chances of getting kidney stones. She also said that there was a great worry about bone loss. You lose your appetite and have a feeling that you can't eat or keep anything down. In her case, she did not eat for four days. Things kind of go topsy-turvy. She said that your face swells, your legs get small, and your hair stands on end. All these changes go on for anywhere from three to five days, and finally, the body adjusts to this new situation, and things become second nature.

Some things get easier immediately. Colonel Collins expressed her wish that her grandmother could have gone to space, because on earth, she was crippled with arthritis and couldn't move her hands. In the environment of outer space, all she would've had to do was to move her fingertips.

I think this astronaut's insights hold significant parallels in regard to systemic church change and the eventual adjustments to a more effortless environment. In my conversations about turnaround churches with women in ministry and Women Married to Men in Ministry, I hear about the difficulties of the adjustment period. Many have gone through the sound barrier, and the sailing is much smoother. And though I'm sure we all would wish for that time to arrive sooner, in the meantime, we can be strengthened by the truths of how the embracing of suffering transforms us so we can be kingdom agents of change to others whom God loves.

As Transformers, We Will Be—
Must Be—Transformed

If there is one stark reality that has surfaced in our collective experiences of radical shifts in our churches, it is this: **The transformer cannot stand apart from the transformation.**

The flight plan we lay out for spiritual renewal in our church becomes a personal journey for our own spiritual maturation. But why does this shake-up seem to affect women in ministry and ministerial families more than it does men? What is it about the unhealthy church systems undergoing a turnaround situation that amplifies our pain and our transition process as women? And what, if anything, can or should we do about this so we can minimize the unnecessary sonic shakings?

When it comes to systemic church change, I don't see in Scripture where women are excused from relationships or responsibilities because of gender. But I just didn't expect to see that women would be disproportionately affected by the results when my husband led the ABCW judicatory toward Great Commission change. Broken relationships inevitably occur through the change and transition processes, and that has been perhaps the biggest source of pain for women in ministry and Women Married to Men in Ministry. Some broken relationships have to happen, maybe (sadly) even most. Perhaps our transformation principles could have been changed or should now be changed. But the results have often proved devastating for many of the women involved.

The radical process needed for church transformation puts us square in the middle of our own gut-wrenching, inescapable challenges and choices. I've reflected long and hard to understand why we're so affected and what to do about it. I have gleaned many insights from other women involved as well as from my research into developmental stages of women and how that affects the ways we usually engage with life.

Why Systemic Change Causes Extra Anguish for Women

I think much of what makes our work as women in systemic change more difficult is that we have not been given the authority to lead but primarily to act as caregivers. In this regard, psychologist Carol Gilligan addresses in her book *In a Different Voice* what may be the core of why change affects women more deeply and differently than it does men. It has to do with at least two issues:

- **How we develop attachments in relationships and define ourselves by those affiliations.**

Women stay with, build on, and develop in a context of attachment and affiliation with others. Indeed women's sense of self becomes very much organized around being able to make, and then to maintain, affiliations and relationships. Eventually, for many women, the threat of disruption of an affiliation is perceived not just as a loss of a relationship but as something closer to a total loss of self.[1]

- **How separation from those relationships—or even the threat of relational disruption—can lead to deterioration of our self-concept.**

Women's perception of social reality centers around experiences of attachment and separation. Life transitions that inevitably engage these experiences can be expected to involve women in a distinctive way. And because women's sense of integrity appears to be intertwined with an ethic of care, so that to see themselves as women is to see themselves in relationship or connection, the major transitions in women's lives would seem to involve changes in the understanding and activities of care.[2]

I don't think our DNA predestines us to be smotherers or martyrs. But it does seem to be a "Fe-male-ness reality" that we have a tendency to waver in our "individuation"—meaning that, for many, perceptions of the self are limited to how others perceive us or how we believe others perceive us. Also, while following Jesus Christ includes a mandate to care for others, codependency occurs when we derive our identity from our relationships instead of from our own sense of self, and, more important, as Christians our identity in Christ.

If it is accurate that some women value connections so much that we will care for others to the detriment of ourselves, then that helps explain some of the emotional complexities observed in turnaround churches. Some women may find it difficult (if not impossible) to dissect self from others or disconnect from caregiving. So, systemic change starts a line of giant dominoes falling, and sometimes they land on us!

- What happens when we've viewed ourselves as *caregiver* (or others view us that way) and suddenly our involvement (or our husband's) with church transition shifts us into the role of *pain giver* to others? Our activities (seemingly) violate our innate ethic of care.
- What happens when those we love in our congregation decide to leave because they don't want to change, can't take any more change, or are in family situations where there is division over commitment to change? (Or, if they do not leave physically, they leave emotionally through anger, depression, or burnout.) Our involvement causes us to lose the very affiliations we so valued.
- What happens if we are at odds with our spouse, family members, parishioners, judicatory leaders, or others about congregational transformation? Our sense of relational separation may lead to feelings of isolation, loss of sense of integration, grieving, and so on.

Compounding these problems are the language and social systems we find ourselves in.

In terms of language, it is far more complex than some simple issue of Men/Mars-versus-Women/Venus. There are underlying perspectives and perceptions that differ radically. As Gilligan describes it, "Research suggests that men and women may speak different languages that they assume are the same, using similar words to encode disparate experiences of self and social relationships. Because these languages share an overlapping moral vocabulary, they contain a propensity for systemic mistranslation, creating misunderstandings which impede communication and limit the potential for cooperation and care in relationships."[3] She concludes that when we assume there is only one mode for interpreting social experience—masculine—instead of two, we reduce the complexity of being human and invalidate the voices of women.

The "Love Languages" concepts developed by Gary Chapman describe similar mistranslations as we attempt to communicate love and caring to others. The kinds of misconnections that happen aren't necessarily due exclusively to differences in gender. If we fail to see the importance of communication cues that are best accepted by the recipients, we miss much that could help us understand human responses to conflict. And this is critical to the context of turnaround churches because conflict is inherent in the process because change is inherent in the process.

In terms of social systems, many denominational traditions undervalue us as women and deflect our voices. Others outright refuse to accept women as ministers or leaders and deny our voices. So, we often walk a tense line. Do we give voice to the reality of our experiences—which maintains our integrity but ultimately risks creating separations—and all that implies? Or, do we say nothing, which may keep us safe but ultimately risks eroding our personhood?

"Dissonant Harmony"—The Paradox of Suffering That Transforms

Picking up the "sonic" part of our transonic flight metaphor, is it even possible to break through the sound barrier of transformation without sending forth a boom? I would suggest that we cannot deal with creating harmony out of change and transition unless we address the discord and shaking of suffering.

In my research for this book, I ran across some early twentieth-century writings by philosopher and author Dane Rudhyar. In an Internet article entitled "Dissonant Harmony: A New Principle of Musical and Social Organization," he presents his view of "dissonant harmony," which is

Not a natural, but a spiritual Harmony; not a basic harmony postulated as a fact from the beginning, but rather Harmony being won every moment of time over conflict and misery, Harmony created out of transfigured suffering. . . . Peace reached through the harmonization of conflicts or rather of differences is obviously of a much richer kind than the peace which is the natural expression of a group of similarities.[4]

Rudhyar did not invent the concept of dissonant harmony—it's been around at least since Renaissance music. However, in his perspective as a philosopher, Rudhyar did cast this concept's implications in terms of a wholistic, spiritual framework. The overall idea that caught my attention was the paradox of how something that "sounds" like it is "off," actually can contribute to something that is right on! And suffering, paradoxically, brings forth transformed character. After all, even Jesus Christ, as the author and completer of our salvation, learned obedience and came to maturity through the things he suffered (Hebrews 2:10). How can we expect to avoid being transformed ourselves when we serve as his agents of transformation? The act of transformation will bring pain and suffering in those who lead. This is an inconvenient unavoidable truth.

Theosophy is a system of thought that can parallel biblical understanding when it helps us keep in tension that, through pain, we gain character. The paradox that sometimes good can be created through something bad (suffering or pain) is very consistent with biblical teaching. This paradoxical approach forces us to balance the tensions in Scripture. When we think of "tension," our minds might go first to the image of tightrope walking, balancing carefully so that we do not fall off *either* this way *or* that way. Certainly, in the beginning stages of church transformations, that image is a reality. In the long run, however, maybe the metaphor of biblical scholar Klyne Snodgrass comes more into play. He likens paradox to the *both/and* kind of tension found in a violin string: both anchored at one end and carefully cinched up at the other so that the string is taut enough to sing the song it came to sing.[5]

The Bible contains many paradoxes, as cultural interpreter Brad Sargent notes:

We who are Western Christians have shown ourselves as *not* being very adept at understanding paradoxes, and yet these enigmas appear all over the New Testament. Jesus Christ is BOTH fully God AND fully human, yet without sin. Christians are BOTH sinners capable of horrific evil and falling short of God's ideal, AND saints capable of bringing immense glory and honor to the God who saved us. We must BOTH die to self AND live unto God in the transformation process. God is BOTH one in essence AND three in person. These seem to be anti-rational conundrums, and yet, are we not more than just a mind? How does the Holy Spirit use our hearts and spirits and emotions and imaginations in accomplishing His will?[6]

Simply put, paradoxes are stumbling blocks to the rational mind that wants everything neatly divided and categorized. If we refuse to reflect on them, paradoxes leave us in dissonance, or they can lead us to devotions and resonance—if we allow God's spirit to work beyond our limited minds and in our whole being through them.

Think of how many both/and setups in Scripture deal with transformation. Put off the old way of life and put on the new. The very thing I don't want to do is exactly what I end up doing; the things I want to do, I don't seem to be able to do. We are decaying day by day in the outer self, while being renewed daily in the inner self.

Another aspect of paradoxes is that two or more things that seem to be contradictory are in fact complementary—they balance each other out. Could this be part of the mystery of why God created man to be in such need of woman, and woman in equal need of man? Through the enmity set forth in the garden after the fall, our destiny is to forever be seeking harmony. Men and women are in so many ways dissimilar, and their relationships are often rife with conflict. Still, in the unification of our opposites we find harmony—in giving and receiving, sharing of giftedness, rejoicing in the glory of the other! And, yes, even through enduring suffering, alone and together.

What human would have conceived of suffering as a catalyst for harmony and resonance? And yet, we find this point and counterpoint repeated in our experiences of brokenness and healing in transformed churches, especially as those who lead themselves find transformation.

Giving Voice 6
Living inside the Pastoral Pressure Cooker

The church I pastor was over 125 years old when I arrived. Coincidently, that was also the average age of the members who were left after many difficult years of decline! Actually, the average age was close to seventy, and I was less than half of that. What were they thinking? What was I thinking?

This church had been prepared as much as possible for growth. Structures that could potentially hinder effectiveness were suspended in favor of streamlined leadership. Improvements were

---

made to the facility before my arrival. The congregation had been coached by a long-term intentional interim to be ready for change. The executive who connected me with the church was confident that within a couple of years, if I did the same turn-around work I had done in my previous church, which caused immediate growth, I could expect to see similar and perhaps greater results. Just plug-and-play.

That was one possibility. I experienced another.

My arrogance did not allow me to see reality clearly. While the structures had changed, the DNA was still 125 years old, and it showed. The changes about which I forewarned the congregation were embraced, but with little numerical results. The church was a lot farther from being vital and vibrant than I realized.

My wife cried herself through the commute to worship every weekend, because it was so pathetic, and it seemed like it would be forever before we would see improvement. She battled depression due to isolation: we had two young children when we arrived, with no friendships or support network. I remember assuring her before the move, "Give me a year, and there will be many young adults we can become friends with."

It was obvious within a few months that I was not going to be able to deliver on that promise. I was failing to provide for her.

I didn't want to realize it at the time, but I had become the pastor of what would become a more traditional turnaround church, where I could expect a seven-year process before feeling like the DNA had shifted and we were growing in the right direction. This was not what my church, my region, my wife, or I signed up for. It was incredibly discouraging to work so hard and see so little tangible return. The faces in the congregation showed the disappointment.

At least for me, I was feeling more and more like a pathetic loser. I had been successful in almost every other venture, and I felt like I was failing. As a man in our culture, I felt the pressures to be successful, which worsened the effect of slow-or-no results.

After about one year, I began to feel numb. I sought out the help of a counselor who helped me identify the fact that I was coming close to falling into depression. My wife, by the way, was already battling depression. We hung together as best we could, feeling very alone and defeated. When you are in this state, you don't reach out to anybody, which, of course, makes you feel all the more alone. It's a vicious cycle.

Of course, I was still pursuing change. And, of course, this created conflict. We lost as many people as we gained in the first few years—read: chips out of my pocket. It carries a high price when long-term members leave the church. Nearly half of my board resigned within a six-month period due to the pressure.

Another staff member's marriage failed, due in part to the stress in this turnaround environment. (Their marriage was not as strong as I thought. They were set up for struggle.) The marriage ended. Before the divorce papers had cooled, my associate was already deep into a relationship that would result in a new marriage within months.

The relationship between myself, the church, and the associate did not end well. A little over a year after my associate resigned, an attempt was made to end my career with false allegations. Gratefully, leadership in my judicatory region and church could clearly see the attack for what it was. They stood with me and my wife as we all moved forward.

Even though I was trying to do the best I could, the pressure resulted in some very poor decisions on my part. Looking back, I just don't think I had the strength or the perspective to make some difficult calls I should have made. Hindsight is always 20/20, I guess.

I can't explain what shifted, but an amazing thing happened after pushing uphill for four years—the cloudbank broke. I don't fully understand the timing, but the DNA had changed more in favor of moving forward. Everybody's DNA changed, including mine. There was a moment when, I think, we all decided to give up on our respective dreams for what we thought things were supposed to look like, and we adopted the unknown but assuredly greater dreams God has for this church. We became one. We became unified in our pursuit of what God wanted to do here.

Everything is different now. There are still challenges, still conflict here and there, still never enough money, not enough volunteers, and so on. But the overall sense of what God is doing here is experienced by all as "wonderful."

My encouragement to any pastor entering into the turnaround environment would be to brace yourself for a potential long haul. Make sure you protect your emotional health. Turnaround work is incredibly complex and emotionally taxing. Much of the work is spent on convincing Christians how to be fully Christian—something nobody admits but is ultimately the reason for a church's decline. You are not a superhero. Without being proactive in this regard, your health, your marriage, and your family will pay the high price for your need to succeed quickly. And the church you serve won't be getting a pastor who is driven solely by the Spirit. You become a barrier because of your blindness to your less-than-holy motivations, and you become deaf to the directing voice of God.

Health is a choice. Choose wisely. Health is a choice. Choose well.

Author's Note: As I have talked with this pastor and observed his life and behavior, he has made significant choices and decisions that have positively affected his health and the health of his family. He has sought counseling, changed his diet and exercise routine, and adjusted his schedule to be more family friendly. Obviously, like all of us, they are a work in progress.

Choice Matters

If paradox occurs when two things that seem contradictory actually do go together, then irony is when two things occur together that really shouldn't. In the midst of the paradox of transformers being transformed, we wrestle with the irony of choices.

We often find ourselves in a catch-22 situation, caught between having options but not wanting to choose and wanting to choose but not having options. Neither one of these so-called "options" is tenable, really. Both are detrimental to our development and our discipleship. But how can we break out of that false dichotomy and find a transformative "third way"?

Barbara would suggest that "choosing not to choose" is more empowering than "reluctance" to choose or "having no choice." Scripture is full of examples of women in untenable positions—is it possible that their personhood was sculpted and revealed in those very circumstances? It's a paradox. These ancient pioneers in breaking the "unsound" barrier faced difficult situations, often brought about through unrighteous behaviors of others (for instance, in the case of Sarah, even her own lying spouse). However, ultimately these circumstances did not impede our foremothers' development and ultimately appear to have strengthened their disciple-ship, as they surrendered as apprentices to the sufferings of Christ.

People used to think that the sound barrier was like an invisible brick wall that would shake and then crumple any plane that attempted to break through it. My own experiences with a decade of immersion obser-vation is that systemic change brings shakings from angst, anguish, and anger. Still, I have also witnessed women glide higher and soar as they realize camaraderie, conviction, and personal changes that bring hope. We must find the hope-filled options that do not compromise our stew-ardship or ourselves but help us break through to some smoothness found only in Mach-10 travel!

SELF-CARE FOR SUCCESS OF WHOLE-PERSON COPILOTS

WINGed Transformation

Whenever change occurs in our life, whether we initiate the change or it is imposed on us by our circumstances, the best place to start is by turning inward and upward—opening our hearts toward God, knowing who we are in Christ without a doubt.

The transforming power of God within enables us to release our fears and concerns. The Spirit allows us to claim our inheritance as a child of the living God and empowers us to be conformed into the likeness of the God in whose image we are made.

We as women, and especially those of us who are Women Married to Men in Ministry, need WINGS—an acronym for Women In Need of Growing Stronger. We need to grow stronger both in God and in ourselves so that we may spread our wings. We earn our wings through the turbulent times by surrendering our will to the "I am." God wants us to be vessels of strength and beauty, inside and out.

God says, "Before I formed you in the womb I knew you" (Jeremiah 1:5). In this case the Hebrew word for *form* means to create or craft. Thus, we can genuinely say that we were crafted as special, unique, and well-thought-out creations of God. Every part of our bodies, our souls (mind, will, emotions), our personalities, and our spirits was created by a Master—an Artisan. We are who God made us to be. Now, the challenge for each of us is to find out how we live within that creation and become the best "me" we can be, to be able to live our best possible life.

How Best to Live as God's Unique Creation

My life's work and ministry have been spent as an entrepreneur. My business was also about transformation. I found that as individuals experienced transformation in their *outward* being, that also affected their *inward* perceptions of themselves.

I, along with my daughter and son, owned a paramedical day spa. We employed twenty-five talented, trained professionals. We served an average of twenty-five hundred clients a month, 95 percent of them women. And these women all expected to *be* better and to *feel* better, so that they could *do* life better. We served women from various spiritual backgrounds, both Christian and others.

We offered a consultation process as one of our services. This included looking at the client as a whole being and assessing various dimensions of life. So, we partnered with physicians, dentists, psychologists, clothing designers, interior designers, artists, and others who could help meet whatever needs the consultation uncovered.

First, my clients would fill out a discovery questionnaire. Then, in my consultant role, I would analyze their facial shape, hair type, body type, coloring, lifestyle activities, and skill level in order to help them be their authentic self. It might sound complicated, but actually, this would simplify life! As we resourced our clients with knowledge and equipped them with relevant skills, they were empowered to make better choices for their lifestyle and personal appearance. They could rid themselves of irrelevant details and decisions. Who wouldn't want that?

And yet, a short while after I began offering this consultation process, I noticed a disturbing trend. Nearly everyone came in with a vision of being like someone else. They would say things like, "I want to look like so-and-so." (You fill in the blank.) "If only I could have her hair, her nose, smile, hips . . ." And on and on it went.

My response was, "You need to *be* the very best you, as everyone else is already taken!" I would remind people of who thought us up and what God said about his creating us: "I know you, I made you special, I created you in time and space." He has committed all his resources into transforming us into his image and created unique opportunities for us to shine for him.

Rules and Roles—or "Real"?

Women Married to Men in Ministry have a position, whether wanted or not. With this position comes an image, a role if you will, and many have been trapped into "pastor's wife" role-playing for a very long time.

It takes courage to step out from behind the role we think we have to maintain and become real. Hopefully, we won't have to wait as long as the Velveteen Rabbit did: until our hair is all rubbed off, our eyes are popping out, and we have become disjointed and shabby! Sooner is better than later.

So, how do we become real? It's about knowing love, by learning to know ourselves and trust ourselves—trust our intelligence, our perspectives, our intuition. It's about finding our voice. Ultimately, it's about knowing who we are in Christ.

This is not a chapter about "how to," as in how to survive illegitimate rules and unrealistic role expectations from those around us. Rather, it is about how to see and perceive the real, deeper issues of our inward beliefs and how to take care of ourselves wholistically in the face of stressful circumstances and faulty stereotypes.

Renewal of Our Minds: Key to "The Real"

Romans 12:2 says, "Do not be conformed to this world, but be transformed by the renewing of your minds, so that you may discern what is the will of God—what is good and acceptable and perfect." Having a renewed mind, from a scriptural perspective, is a mind that is so saturated with the word of God that when a crisis hits, rather than relying on our wits for a solution to the crisis, we rely upon God's word.

Our mind is an amazing thing. It holds the ability to reason, to remember, to describe, to classify, to solve problems, and to dream dreams. Our mind consists of our fears, hopes, values, behaviors, prejudices, perceptions, and attitudes. But the mind also needs something else—a continuing process of transformation to renew life and thought. I am at the beginning of becoming saturated with God's word and my mind is being renewed. I do still try to figure everything out more often than I should, but I am in the process of transformation, as are you!

I've come to see that this transforming process generally develops through pain of some kind. This transition can come through many forms. Sometimes it arrives when we embrace the crisis-plus-opportunity of a change process. For instance, I have a friend who regularly practices this principle of transformation of the mind; she reached this only through a painful process of dealing with a troubled child. Each of us has something unique that can spark such renewal—especially when we are women on a mission to break through the sound barrier with a turnaround church! But, regardless of our specific situations, renewing of the mind always involves the empowering spirit of God, working through God's word, to conform us to the image of Christ.

If our heads are not changed (that is, our thinking renewed), then we will toy with only the perceptions of Scripture and tradition that confirm our prior values and commitments. By the renewing of our minds (that is, getting our heads changed), we can think clearly, see the absolute priority of the gospel, and be changed by the experience. Once again, "no pain, no gain."

A Ministry of "Letting Go"

The demands upon change ministers are great. These circumstances create a pressurized situation that requires all of our focus, energy, and strength for an extended period of time. As a result, we receive the opportunity for a ministry of "letting go." Perhaps this is what some older hymns and sermons refer to as "surrender." Others may use the term *relinquish*—meaning to give something over to God, not give up on it. Letting go is a kingdom sacrifice—both for us as individuals and for our family, if we are married or parents. It requires a unique mind-set of trust (or at least willingness to learn how to trust God) in order to accomplish it.

Through observation and reading Scripture, I observed the principle that significant kingdom ministry comes only out of extraordinary sacrifice, perseverance, determination, and a passion for obedience to the gospel. In other words, we grow with a steep learning curve. I see much "letting go" on the part of women in Scripture. Also, in looking at the lives of early missionaries, it is obvious that the women involved had the gift of letting go as well.

I've often wondered about contemporary Women Married to Men in Ministry, such as Ruth Bell Graham, the wife of the evangelist Billy Graham, whether they have the gift of "letting go." If so, much of the child rearing and other responsibilities of daily life were done on her own.

Giving Voice 7
Starting at a New Venue with a Change Approach

Romans 8:28 says, "We know that all things work together for good for those who love God, who are called according to his purpose." The operative words here are *all* and *called*. That is a verse I have held on to through many difficult times. It has allowed me to put painful circumstances of our ministry into an eternal perspective that has then allowed me to accept the effects of our calling to seek and save the lost of this world.

My story begins with a calling by God in my life. Had I not felt that direct call with his divine direction in my life, I don't know if I would have had the courage—much less desire—to stick it out through some very dark times.

My husband had been a pastor for several years in a system that provided a lot of security. He had been feeling God calling him in a different direction. He was willing to leave what he knew to be a secure future in order to follow God fully wherever that might lead him. That was the only way to be able to fully realize his passion for people who are lost. That desire to be obedient to God's call tested what we really believed about doing whatever it takes to reach people for Christ, including the sacrifice of some very dear relationships.

In our initial interview in the church where we now serve, God spoke to both my husband and me very clearly that this is where he wanted us to serve him. No question about it! Even though I was very scared about leaving the security we then enjoyed, I could not deny that God had spoken. There were a few bumps in the road to the final destination, but the assurance of God's call in our life was undeniable and unstoppable. I can't even tell you how important that assurance of his calling has been. We were aware of the fact that my husband was not the church members' first choice for their pastor, but looking back on it, our knowing was crucial to our understanding that we are where God, not just man, has called us. We will stay here until God calls us elsewhere.

When our church started growing, many people resisted. Not so much the new people, but the changes that it took to attract them. When we arrived, there were about seventy regular attenders, mostly of retirement age. There were about five children, three of whom were ours. When friends would come to visit and see our congregation, they would see what God did not allow us to see. We were so excited about what we knew God was going to do in this place, we could not see the obvious obstacles.

We were welcomed with open arms. We were given friendship and generous gifts. A family we did not know even loaned us a lot of money to buy a house that we would not have been able to afford. We felt loved and excited! However, those feelings were short-lived.

As my husband made more changes that needed to happen, people resisted more forcefully. He was called evil, and he was even asked to resign—actually, a signed petition demanded his resignation. I could not believe how misunderstood he had become. It was very painful for me, and I cried a lot (a great weight loss plan that I wouldn't recommend). I was afraid to go to the mailbox, for fear there would be another mass mailing that criticized my husband and the way he was doing things. A mass exodus occurred and out walked many of our friends and most of the givers of the church. This was certainly not what we had signed up for! But God was so good. He showed us the new believers who were so thankful that there was now a "church for people who don't like church," where they had come to know about God's love for them and his desire for them to know him more.

For me personally, being the pastor's wife has been a difficult position to be in. Often, it is my husband's decisions that affect my friendships in painful ways. Friends who have loved us, prayed for us, supported us, celebrated with us have walked away from us. That kind of rejection is never easy to deal with. It was unbearable at times, and the cost has been great. I trust people less as the years go on, and I fear investing in friends because they may leave some day.

Still, God is great all the time. In light of eternity and the great work for the kingdom that I see daily at our church these days, I can count the cost worth it. Weekly attendance at our church now runs over one thousand and we have families of all ages with kids galore! It has been a difficult path to walk, but a necessary one. I often wish I was not the one chosen to walk it, but wait— his faithfulness through it all has helped me grow into the person I now am, with the ability to trust God even more.

"Breathing Space" So We Can Fly

As we move toward Mach-10 ministry, we will have many opportunities to try out new ways of thinking and behaving. This is a process, so we need to be patient with ourselves, allow ourselves sufficient breathing space. This is essential because, as one mature woman in ministry whose husband is also in ministry stated, "Being on the front lines of this war of change sucked the air right out of my lungs!" If that is true for someone who is mature both chronologically and spiritually, what impact must radical paradigm shifts have on young women with young families involved in ministry?

To survive the culture shock of change, we definitely need to comply with some rules, just as the flight attendants forewarn, "In case of emergency, put your own oxygen mask on first before you try to assist others." If we have no air in our spiritual lungs, we cannot give voice to what's in our hearts.

In fact, no breath means death! Breath is the biblical metaphor for the Holy Spirit. God breathed on us in the beginning, giving us the breath of life. The Holy Spirit gives power to resist a life of conformity and instead undergo transformity to the image of Christ. This is critical truth! For years, we have been taught and trained to be conformers. The way of the world, the "American Way," and even many (or most) church cultures attempt to squeeze us into their molds of how to behave, perform, and appear. We come to believe we always need to "fit in," to do what is expected. With compliance, we get their seal of approval and confirmation in conformity.

And yet, the word of God is about transforming, not conforming. If we have no breathing space to find his freedom, we cannot help others find release into who they were designed to be so that they can do what God created them to do. Knowing God and knowing ourselves will help us speak the truth in love. Knowing we live only to please the one and only living God will give us the freedom to truly spread our wings and fly.

My grandmother, a strong woman, was an entrepreneur before the word was being used. She was a woman who knew how to fly. She was my mentor, the woman who helped me find my voice, and she is the reason I am a believer in Jesus Christ today.

As a child, I watched and listened while she and my grandfather served in the church. I remember clearly all the challenges that eventually evolved into a church split—a heartbreaking event, then and now. My grandmother continued serving without complaint. Through this, she taught me about not being conformed but being transformed for a greater and higher purpose through these painful experiences. She always had her eye on the sky. I can still hear her out-of-tune voice, singing with the purest vision of longing. Perhaps we, too, can take hope in the words of one of her favorite songs, "I'll Fly Away."

> Some glad morning when this life is o'er,
> I'll fly away;
> To a home on God's celestial shore,
> I'll fly away.
> I'll fly away, O Glory,
> I'll fly away;
> When I die, Hallelujah, by and by,
> I'll fly away.
> Just a few more weary days and then,
> I'll fly away;
> To a land where joys shall never end,
> I'll fly away.[1]

We will one day fly away—no aircraft needed. We will no longer be heavier than air! But until then, we will need to concern ourselves with what sometimes weighs us down.

Effects of the "Stress Response"

What follows may be the most prescriptive sections of *Women Married to Men in Ministry*. Since they detail many aspects of self-care, they could also be the most necessary. Let me begin with some of the fascinating things I discovered in my research on the early years of the space program.

In the beginning, astronauts were put to the test physically in almost every way conceivable. They were poked, prodded, and X-rayed. Time and time again they were spun, submerged, and entombed. They were repeatedly advised to put off having a family in case they were called to duty. These thirteen *female* pilots who trained in secret managed to pass the grueling physical examination for astronauts in the early 1960s, proving that they indeed had as much of "the right stuff" as the men chosen for the Mercury 7 program. Even today, the existence of these women and their Mercury 13 program is a little-known fact. These women had to be in prime condition in order to reach for the moon, literally.

And, so do we, as women in ministry or Women Married to Men in Ministry, if we want to soar into the stratosphere of service. It's no picnic, preparing ourselves to weather the three, five, seven years of intense shaking that are likely before we break through the sound barrier of radical church turnaround. But, it is essential that we develop our strength, energy, courage, and perseverance to withstand. We need to be in the best possible condition—body, soul, and spirit.

How can we prepare ourselves for such a task as this? How can we balance our lives in such a way that we are able to honor God and have a successful life as well as a successful ministry?

Christian psychiatrist Marion T. Nelson has stated that being a Woman Married to a Man in Ministry is the most hazardous and dangerous occupation a woman can have. In an informal, unscientific study I conducted, I discovered that Women Married to Men in Ministry deal with significant numbers and levels of health conditions. (Eight out of every ten women I spoke to deal with health issues such as fibromyalgia, migraine headaches, stress disorders, eating disorders, and depression.)

Mostly these women are overextended and completely exhausted trying to do it all, with little regard for their own needs of body, soul, and spirit. The Scriptures are clear that we are the temple of God to be honored. However, that seems to be a last-resort activity when everything else is done—which is almost never. And here I am speaking out of my own experience, not just my observations of others.

Being involved with systemic ministry change and the resulting transition is very demanding and stressful. When we experience excessive stress—whether from internal worry and anxiety or at external circumstances—a bodily reaction is triggered called the fight-or-flight response. God apparently hardwired this response into our brain to improve our chances of survival in any dangerous confrontation. When our fight-or-flight response is activated, a sequence of nerve firings occurs, and chemicals like adrenaline and cortisol are released into our bloodstream. This rush of chemical changes causes our body to undergo dramatic changes. Our awareness intensifies. Our heart pounds, and our pulse increases. Our immune system mobilizes with increased activation.

When these protective systems are engaged, we tend to perceive everything in our environment as a possible threat to our survival. Thus, by its very nature, the fight-or-flight systems bypass our rational mind and move us intuitively into protection mode. So, where do we go when, humanly speaking, we have no one to fight for us in our fight and nowhere safe to fly in our flight? That is typically the case of Women Married to Men in Ministry. This means the continual and extraordinary stresses of radical changes leave us vulnerable to a vicious fight-or-flight cycle.

Our bodies cannot withstand constant high-alert status. Eventually the stress will affect our health negatively as it puts us in a place of fear and narrows our focus to those things that can harm us. This wired-in response has a cumulative effect of building up stress hormones, which are not properly metabolized over time. This in turn can result in disorders of the nervous system, headaches, irritable bowel syndrome, high blood pressure, and the like. Disorders of the hormone and the immune systems create susceptibility to infection, chronic fatigue, depression, and heart disease, and such autoimmune diseases as rheumatoid arthritis, lupus, and allergies.

Circling Back Toward Better Health

We can learn important things from the life of Christ in regard to our health and wholeness. According to Luke 2:52, "Jesus grew in wisdom [mind] and stature [body], and in favor with God [Spirit] and men [relationships]" (NIV). In the common recovery language of today, we might say that Jesus had access to high IQ (intelligence quotient), EQ (emotional quotient), and SQ (social quotient).

This gives us a picture of wholistic health. God is concerned with us as a whole person. The scripture cited shows us that God sees a person complete—not as an isolated being, but as someone living in relationship with God and other people and self.

In the biblical tradition, a human being is a living person, a unity of body and soul. When persons were in relationships with God, they were in a state of shalom—health, wholeness, and peace. Persons who were whole had salvation. Here, salvation is viewed not just as a spiritual or physical state, but in a whole context that encompasses our entire triune being of body, soul, and spirit.

If we do not have our health, we have very little else. The quality of our life is diminished—and likely, so is the quantity. It seems the churched community clings to the idea that taking care of ourselves is a selfish act. In reality, self-care is a very selfless thing to do so that we are able to be available to the ministry in which God has called us. It is essential that we master some methods for controlling our stress responses.

Certainly the place to start is by going to God in prayer and using his word as medicine to help reassure us of his protection. Additional disciplines that some women in ministry have found helpful in conquering stress are biofeedback, hypnosis, massage, and the relaxation response technique. There are many resources available on these specific approaches. So, in the meantime, I'd like to suggest seven basic health-care principles that work together in synergy to help us deal with stress.

1. *Good Nutrition.* We need a balance of vitamins, minerals, complex carbohydrates, fat, and protein. Hippocrates, the father of medicine, said, "Let your food be your medicine." The Bible says that no one lives by bread alone but by every word that proceeds from the mouth of God. So, taking in good nutrition physically can bridge us to taking in good nutrition from God's word.

Brenda Watson, a naturopathic doctor, colon therapist, public speaker, author, teacher, and product creator talks, in her PBS special, about our body needing four critical items that can be obtained in the food we eat or in food supplements. She used the acronym H.O.P.E. for them:

- **H**igh fiber—from complex carbohydrates as in vegetables and fruits and grains
- **O**mega-3 oil—obtained through eating salmon
- **P**robiotics—found in live-culture yogurt
- **E**nzymes—help us digest food and moderate inflammation. In the Jewish culture, sauerkraut or dill pickles may be eaten prior to a meal to increase hydrochloric acid and stimulate enzyme production for digestion.

These are suggestions for you to consider. Please consult your doctor before changing your diet.

2. *Hydration.* The body is up to 70 percent water. Did you know that dehydration causes mental and emotional stress, but that stress also causes dehydration? It's a vicious cycle! So, keeping our body hydrated with high-quality H_2O is of the utmost importance. Dr. Don Colbert recommends that we consume half of our body weight (in ounces) every day. So, if you weigh 160 pounds, you should consume 80 ounces of water. He also recommends sipping only a half cup of water every half-hour, never chugging, to avoid washing important minerals out of the body.[2] One should stop drinking a few hours before bed to avoid having to visit the bathroom in the middle of the night and disrupting the sleep cycle.

Everyone can benefit from drinking more water, but please check with your doctor before increasing your intake significantly.

3. Exercise. To give us a strong heart, experts recommend exercising at least three times a week to elevate our heart rate. A good one-mile prayer walk will help body, soul, and spirit. Some say we need to walk ten thousand steps a day or the equivalent of four miles. To increase flexibility, do a series of thirty-second stretches. To stretch the entire body should take about fifteen minutes a day. It develops the body's ability to handle stress, helps manage adrenaline, and builds endorphins that make us feel more upbeat. Of course, it also benefits our bones, muscles, and connective tissues. Be sure to check with your doctor for an approved exercise routine.

4. Deep Breathing. We need to bring oxygen into the body to fuel our cells and our brain and to reduce stress. Oxygen destroys pathogens, bacteria, viruses, parasites, and fungi. When oxygen levels increase, so do endorphins, which are natural mood balancers. Oxygen balances the blood chemistry in ways that allow toxins to be removed more quickly, pumps up the immune system, and begins to lift anxiety. We need to bring our awareness to our breathing and what affects it. For instance, we need to be careful about foods we eat, as there is an inverse proportion between fats, sugars, and proteins and oxygen—the more of these we eat, the lower the oxygen in our system. Also, I find stress causes us to hold our breath.

5. Sleep. We need six to eight hours of deep sleep nightly for physical renewal. It is recommended that the sleep cycle should start no later than 10:00 p.m. If you have difficulty sleeping (as I do), this could be a result of an imbalance of hormones, as well as other difficulties, one of which is worry. Also, we should consider whether or not to watch a disturbing TV show or even news programs, as these are mostly bad news and they can get our adrenaline going. I find that reading Scriptures in the evening can be very helpful for stimulating a peaceful sleep in the Lord. Sometimes a magnesium supplement or warm milk before going to bed is also helpful. There are other products you might want to investigate. They are special nighttime B-complex vitamins, the herb valerian root, holy basil, and a product called Theanine Serene produced by Source Naturals (this is a calming complex). These are not recommendations, they are only suggestions for you to investigate. Be sure to check with your doctor before beginning any supplements as they can also have adverse health effects.

6. Sabbath Rest. Everyone needs a margin, a time for reflecting and refreshing. Since Sunday is typically a workday for us, we need to set aside a weekday for rest and recreation. And a note: running errands is not considered resting! In addition to a weekly day of rest, it helps to plan some "God time" on a daily basis for prayer, meditation, and relaxation.

7. Care of Our Physical Appearance. I recommend we take a red marker and mark a red-letter day on our calendar. This is our special day to take care of ourselves and our physical appearance needs, whether it's one time a week or one time a month. This should be outside of our daily routines, of course.

Survival Kit for Combating Stress

Here are other tidbits and techniques to consider for our survival kit in maintaining momentum toward Mach-10 ministry:

- Body massages build up the immune system and have great stress-relieving benefits.
- We need to have flexibility of mind as well as flexibility in the body. So, it helps to develop our curiosity and become lifelong learners.
- We need to be mindful and pay attention to our thoughts and our feelings because they lead to our beliefs and our actions.
- We need to resolve issues by listening to God's voice and finding our voice and communicating our needs.
- Practice forgiveness—this is very difficult for most people and can only be accomplished through relationship with God through Christ and a perseverance and determination to obey his word.
- Develop healthy relationships—ask God to help you create the friendships that he would want you to have instead of doing friendship out of a sense of obligation.
- Nurture our relationship with God through the practice of listening; this builds up the "muscles of our spiritual ears."
- Knowing God through his attributes gives us confidence in him.
- Developing spiritual discipline will come through knowing God.
- Determine to believe and obey God's word above our feelings and beliefs.
- Create a "SOAP" Life Journal—SOAP stands for: Scripture (write out one verse), Observation (what does it mean?), Application (to my life), Prayer (respond to God).

CHAPTER TEN

FLIGHT TEAMS AND A VIEW FROM SPACE

The Rest of the Story: What Was on the Note?

D o you remember this from the introduction about the hijacking? What was on the note? What saved the day? What was it that united or reunited a group of cotravelers and emboldened them with courage to regain control and move back to the original Great Commission flight plan?

This is what was scrawled on the note:

The time is now.

We must move ahead, as commanded.

We could lose our life, but if we don't fight evil, many more will die.

If not now, when? If not you and me, who?

The signal is, "MOVE OUT." Hear the voice. Follow—obey.

It's the only way.

We are in this together.

Since we are in this together, it's important to think through who the "we" are on our flight team and run through some last instructions before takeoff.

Care and Church Care

There are multiple fronts in which we can expand our aeronautics analogy of wings. Wings will help us keep our balance so we can fly as we were meant. We need wings of both:

- Healthy church *and* healthy ministerial family.
- Men *and* women partnering together in leadership.
- Self-care *and* church care for us as ministers.

I'd like to zoom in for a bit more detailed look at the last pair on that list, as this book prepares to land and you prepare for takeoff into the future.

When the change process was introduced in our region, no one had any idea of how long it would take to reset a church's focus on the Great Commission. Now we know it usually takes from three to five years, and in some cases, up to seven years. It is not easy, at any rate. However, we find that leaders can better endure for this season when we know that it's for important eternal purposes. And the pattern we have found is that smooth air will eventually come.

Even when we have a godly motivation and focus, we cannot predict or control our emotional responses to the heavy spiritual shaking that we encounter in the gap. The ministers in our region experienced a broad spectrum of feelings through the change and transition processes here: living in the shadow, crisis of neglect, identity crisis, ministry comparisons, intense loneliness. These feelings arise both from what's happening around us and from what's happening within us.

For dealing with the feelings, my recommendation for self-care has been to seek and stick with a qualified counselor who is **not** generally connected within one's denominational or relational circles. For those who are married, self-care could also involve both spouses working to open up lines of communication in which to process the complications of ministry and living in relationship. These options provide a safe place in which to find our voices and express our needs. This keeps it real: what good or how real is a seemingly successful ministry without a truly successful marriage?

Another area we need to consider is church care. It may seem self-indulgent to say that we need to communicate our needs and boundaries clearly to our congregation. However, if we are called into a plateaued or declining congregation, there are inevitably church-culture reasons for their current status. So, we need to explore how to shift faulty stereotypes and any other ill-conceived cultural aspects that prove consumerist and poisonous.

Kingdom Flight Safety Systems: Teams, Tools, and Rules

"Safety First" is more than a mission statement at SkyWest Airlines—it's a way of life. SkyWest's impeccable safety record spans more than 30 years. It begins with the highest caliber of trained professionals and extends to a proven fleet of aircraft.

Each day, thousands of SkyWest employees are responsible for the safety of hundreds of thousands of passengers. SkyWest's experienced mechanics, pilots, flight attendants, and ground personnel have the know-how and ability to keep their passengers safe.

—SkyWest Airlines

When we board a commercial flight, we want to know that we'll be safe and that we'll get to our destination. Kingdom air flights share the same goals as those listed above. In fulfilling the Great Commission and breaking the sound barrier, it is key that we conduct safe travel toward the predetermined destination and that we do this by proper means—the right "flight rules" and quality equipment.

A number of elements work together to create safety systems for both commercial and kingdom flights, and people are behind every element. The following categories of people are meant to work together as a team. Exclude any part of the overall team or reduce the necessary attention to their roles and rules, and flights automatically become far more risky.

Pilots and First Officers. Extensive training is required to become a pilot. This includes ground school, flight simulator experience, numerous hours of supervised flight, safety trainings, and so on—and annual required update trainings. Fitness for flight requires not only rigorous skill training but also regular, comprehensive medical examinations. Pilots and first officers must also maintain physical and mental wellness, and their vision is tested periodically.

Are those piloting our plane maintaining the wholistic health needed? Are they receiving critical update trainings on a regular basis to keep current with the times?

Flight Attendants. Onboard flight team members focus on maintaining safety first, then service. Flight attendants undergo intensive training in safety and security, which includes protocols and procedures for emergency situations. They must pass recertification tests for first aid annually.

Do our stewards know how to administer "spiritual CPR" in emergency situations? Are they equipped for general service to meet basic needs for passenger comfort and safety?

Aircraft Mechanics. At SkyWest, each plane receives attention from a mechanic every day, standard servicing every third day, thorough servicing and inspection every fifth day, extensive maintenance every fifty-four days, and a complete overhaul every 540 days. Aircraft mechanics take an initial three years of schooling for certification plus an additional three weeks of training every two years.

Who serves on our Safe Flight Team as a mechanic, doing routine assessment to see what needs to be tuned up or overhauled? Are they trained to work on the kind of aircraft we are using, or are they attempting to tinker with machines they aren't equipped for?

Ground Personnel. You wouldn't necessarily think that people who work on the tarmac team would need extensive training, but they do. This includes both classroom and on-the-job training in safety issues, such as practices for loading and unloading luggage without causing damage to the cargo or injuries to themselves. Ground personnel are also responsible for running various pieces of equipment, navigating the aircraft in and out of the gates, and deicing planes when needed to ensure safe takeoff. So, their roles in creating a safe flight team are just as critical, though not as visible.

Who is on our team to ensure all the right material gets to the right places at the right times and that people are directed to where they need to go? Who can take care of critical needs caused by changes in "cultural weather"?

Flight Control. Those who dispatch aircraft and serve as system controllers and customer service coordinators play vital roles in keeping flights safe. All undergo extensive training related to their particular areas of work. Dispatchers oversee fuel plans, configure route selections according to Federal Aviation Administration guidelines and weather analysis (they train in meteorology), and monitor flights. System controllers take care of coordinating flights to ensure the smooth flow of air traffic. They deal with flight cancellations and delays, adherence to flight schedules, and optimization of all related operations. Customer service coordinators assist the system controllers and act as advocates for customers—always keeping the needs of passengers in mind. While there may be parallels to flight control personnel within a local church, the analogy seems to fit more with the staff and resources offered through denominations and judicatories.

What congregational or transformational emergencies are of our own making as leaders? as congregation members? as denominational workers? What navigation tools and safety systems are provided by our judicatory/denomination? How does time figure into our plans—is this about speed, sustainability, both, or something else? How could consultants help us optimize our plans in prejourney, launching, in-flight assessments and corrections, and so on? What kinds of consultants would be the most helpful? How do we ensure that there is a vehicle to take the next generation of fliers to the right destination, and where does the denomination/judicatory fit in with that need? Do we really need "clearance" for our flight, and if so, where does ultimate authorization come from?

The Safety Department. Some team members function almost completely behind the scenes, but their roles are crucial for maintaining the big-picture perspective of safety in the airline systems. Those in the Safety Department oversee implementation of all safety requirements and conduct periodic assessments and "safety audits." They solicit suggestions from pilots and others for improving the level of safety in the system. In the United States, they also serve in liaison roles between the airline, the Department of Transportation, and the Federal Aviation Administration.

How are our liaison relationships with other churches in our area, other churches in our denomination, and staff in our judicatory? How do our denominational executives seek input for improving the level of safety in our church and judicatory systems?

Customer Service. Those who work in airline customer service—check-in agents, ticket takers, managers—along with flight attendants, present more of the public face of an airline than do any other team members. Being listed last does not mean these are the least important. Their work involves mostly up-front interaction with people. As gatekeepers, they meet us whenever we have transition points in our travels—check-in, departure, arrival, connecting flight directions. If they are grouchy, cold, or indifferent, their demeanor is often taken as the spirit of the entire enterprise.

Who in our congregation is the most present to new travelers and old? Whose face is the most memorable among us? Is that good, or not so good, and what can we do to improve the quality of our presence with those traveling on this spiritual journey with us?

Flight Rules and Tools. Airlines are required to: file a flight plan with the authorities, get clearance for the flight so it does not interfere with other planes, take off under guidance, stay in contact with air-traffic controllers, stay on course, listen to air-traffic reports on changing weather conditions and unexpected incidents, and land under guidance. Sustainability for making repeated flights requires: maintenance plans, maintenance experts and workers, inside cleanup, and periodic equipment checks for accuracy.

Elements of navigation include using maps, charts, latitude and longitude to specify precise locations, plotting tools (straightedge, dividers to measure distances, compass, protractor for measuring angles), landmarks (visual cues), radar (audio cues), compass bearings and current position, chronometer, Global Positioning System (to triangulate location from signals provided by twenty-four earth-orbiting satellites), and gyroscope (to determine precise direction of the flight). (Other books in the Growing Healthy Churches series address many of these aspects, though not in the aeronautics metaphor.[1])

What tools, assessments, and systems are we using to ensure an accurate and relevant flight plan? Are there methods and means we could add or change to make our flight plans better and more strategic?

Team Mismatches and Missed Methods

This is all great in theory. But what about in practice? How did we get to the place where so many in our denominations and congregations function in inappropriate or unwanted roles in kingdom flight plans?

On our team, do we have mismatches or missed methods?

- Do we have pilots who refuse to direct the plane to the right destination? Or, do they refuse to have a flight crew?
- Do we have women who are capable, gifted, trained, and pilot-worthy and want to be pilots or copilots but have been assigned to duties as flight attendants instead?
- Do we have Women Married to Men in Ministry who would be quite content to serve as ticket takers or flight attendants but who are triangulated into situations as if they were the pilot or copilot?

- Do our denominational executives remain far off, often serving as air-traffic controllers (which is fine and needed), but oops! Did anyone arrange for flight mechanics to do regular assessments and maintenance to ensure the plane can fly?
- Do our congregation members act like passengers instead of stewards? Do they assume that the people who are actually supposed to pilot the plane are their personal flight attendants?
- Do people who are not congregants try out the flight as passengers, or are we flying an empty plane? Do these passengers disembark at a connecting point before the destination we're scheduled to take them to? If so, how could we help them continue aboard and consider this as a connecting flight to a destination farther than they may have originally anticipated?
- Congregants should all be available as ticket takers, flight attendants, and so on. Some might eventually become head stewards, or even go to flight school to become (co)pilots. Somebody has to take care of the assessments—and don't forget to get people in the air-traffic-control towers!

How to Forge a Fantastic "Flight Team"

Church transformation is a complex but important aspect of kingdom service. To get our "airplanes" up and running with mature, trained pilots, all key players need to know how they can best contribute to the team.

Here are some suggestions for current "best practices" to implement and "foresightful practices" to develop. Some address more the personal or professional aspects of teamwork; however, these realms are not separate, though they may be distinct. What we do in one realm of our life affects all others, for better or for worse. So, the following are given with the hope that we will pursue all that are relevant, in order to become the best we can be, wholistically.

Denominations/Judicatories

General Suggestions. Honor the use of women's gifts and talents within the church. Provide opportunities for women to grow in their maturity and skills. Include women in most training exercises and offer substantive sessions for Women Married to Men in Ministry at events where spouses are invited. Set up, endorse, and resource a network for WoMen-toring—women mentoring women. Provide opportunity and environment for women to connect naturally.

Preplacement Process. Include in interview processes the Woman Married to the Man in Ministry. Talk openly about expectations of him and her as a ministry couple up front. Do not give couples an opportunity to make a leadership commitment based on incomplete knowledge.

Early into a New Pastorate. Six to nine months after the minister is in place, have a "Great Expectations" meeting that includes the spouse. Talk about realistic expectations and get everything out in the open about this and next stages of ministry work. Communicate the cost of change, offer hope, and give realistic time frames to accomplish the goals of transformation in the church.

Personal and Professional Development. Offer opportunities to both pastors and spouses for training in change and transition management as well as ongoing coaching and counseling. Acknowledge pastors, spouses, and ministerial families regularly; recognize them with personal thanks, words of esteem, and tangible tokens of appreciation.

Maintaining Healthy Family Systems. Resource ministerial families with books, CDs, tapes, training funds, and so on, that will strengthen their members' maturity, skills, and family systems. Resource, adequately fund, and enthusiastically promote pastor, spouse, and ministerial family support services. Outsource or review and provide quality resources for wholistic health issues involving body, soul, and spirit.

Women in Ministry and Women Married to Men in Ministry

Health and Growth. Find out who you are so you can be yourself; find out who you are in Christ so you can become your best self. Commit to becoming a healthy, growing, mature disciple of Jesus Christ. Value self-development, self-care, and health care. Schedule times out for restoration and refreshment. Take advantage of opportunities that develop various dimensions of personhood, especially when you can connect with other women as part of a support network.

Roll with Your Roles. Know the costs involved with systemic change within the church; consider your roles in transformation and embrace them. Study and rethink the information regarding picking up your cross and following Christ. Consider how suffering fits into the big picture of making disciples for Christ. Participate in as many of the training events as possible and in the networking and support services offered. In order to receive support, you must show up—and you must speak up if your needs are not being met.

Invest in Our Future. Be intentional in leaving a legacy for those who follow, especially by role-modeling maturity and ministry for other women. If you have children, do not neglect your priority to them so they, too, can become healthy, growing, mature disciples of Jesus.

Consider all of the suggestions below, if you are also involved in a more professional ministry role, whether paid or unpaid.

Women in Ministry

Training and Support. Have vision and passion for the work of transformational change. Become as equipped as possible for the rigors of this work. Maintain an accountability relationship with at least one peer who *is not* part of the church you serve.

Professional Development. Training clusters that would be especially helpful for transformation ministry work include:

- Information about new paradigms, systemic change, transition, and how to communicate such transformational work within denominational and church circles.
- Insight into organizational systems, leadership, empowerment, delegation, volunteer mobilization, appropriate intrachurch communication, and church discipline.
- Coaching for personal presentation and image, voice training—improving the voice's resonance and quality and protecting it from misuse and overuse.

Husband/Pastor

Follow the suggestions on Health and Growth, Roll with Your Roles, Invest in Our Future, Training and Support, and Professional Development in the sections for Women in Ministry and Women Married to Men in Ministry. Parallel principles apply!

Marriage. Value, recognize, and thank your spouse on a regular basis. Communicate daily with your spouse about life and work, losses and joys. Be cautious so you do not share sensitive or confidential matters that should remain at work and not go into the home.

Family Systems. Consciously and conscientiously count the cost of systemic change on the family unit. Schedule separate times out with your spouse and with family on a regular basis. Protect the integrity of the ministerial spouse and family relationships by maintaining appropriate boundaries; do not allow congregational and denominational needs to erode ministerial family systems. (See list under Church Congregation Members following.)

Church Congregation Members

We assume those in ministry choose that profession because they want to lead and serve others by equipping them to fulfill the Great Commission. This role still carries many unspoken expectations, and there are persistent demands on the time and energy of those in ministry, their spouses, and their families. Congregation members need to be considerate toward their leaders, especially in seeking to honor and bless them. Sincerity and a willingness to serve are truly appreciated! It is best to ask how you may be of help, and give ministers and their spouses the opportunity to communicate what they are comfortable or not comfortable with.

Basic Boundaries. Protect the integrity of the ministerial marriage and family in the same ways that you want for your own situation. Always call ahead and set a time to visit, never just drop by the ministry family's home. When calling, ask if it's a good time to talk, and keep it brief. Schedule a more convenient time to call if it is not a good time. Respect the ministry family's time for dinner, family time, and bedtimes by not calling then unless it is a dire emergency. Honor your pastor's time off.

Respectfulness. Respect the privacy of the pastor's home. Ask the Woman Married to a Man in Ministry how she would like to be introduced to others. Many do not want to be called "The Pastor's Wife." They have a name and interests of their own. They have their own ministry and calling and prefer to be recognized for themselves, not solely identified by their husband's position. Remind others to remember to appreciate the Woman Married to a Man in Ministry as a woman in her own right.

Appreciation. Offer ministers, spouses, and their families words of affirmation and appreciation. This can take many forms: affirmative words spoken on a Sunday, cards and e-mails (thinking of you, birthday, thank you), praying and telling them you are praying. Appreciate the fact that ministers, spouses, and families need uninterrupted time away, whether vacation, retreat, or holidays.

Serving Those Who Serve. Those in ministry need to have a life too. Find ways to serve that give them some free time; check to see if your idea or activity would be needed, timely, or appreciated. Babysit or provide funds for sitters, run errands, work on the inside or outside of their home in ways that are according to their liking and taste, and, on their request, provide meals (be considerate of dietary and health needs and preferences).

Blessing with Gifts. Gifts large and small are a great way to show appreciation and strengthen relationships. Consider gift certificates/cards as possibilities for: *personal care* (a day away, manicure, facial, massage, pedicure), *specialty stores* (videostore, bookstore, gourmet food, restaurant), *other goods and services* (housecleaning two times a year, prepaid gas card or telephone card). Possibilities for other goodies are endless: covering travel and fees for a conference, a basket of bath and beauty products, pasta fixings, a complete picnic, magazine subscription (such as to *Just Between Us*, for women in ministry and Women Married to Men in Ministry). Consider offering something and letting them pick among the options. Never offer a hand-me-down or hand-me-over unless it is something exceptionally special or needed, as expressed by the ministry couple.

Developing Those Who Serve. Provide an educational fund yearly for the Woman Married to the Man in Ministry to pursue areas of her own interest or need, to benefit both her and the church. *This should be a line item in the yearly budget.*

My Hope for Us:
Last Words before Takeoff

As I mentioned earlier, astronautics scientist Wernher von Braun once stated that theoretically the natural laws of the universe are so precise and predictable that we have no difficulty building a spaceship, sending a person to the moon, and timing the landing with the precision of a fraction of a second.

And yet, the exploration needed within the "inner space" of the human heart seems less predictable. However, we can still break the sound barrier with well-applied principles of mission, vision, values, strategies, tactics, leadership, and interventions. These allow us to overcome the inertness of a wounded or hardened heart or a dying or dead church.

My hope is that all involved in the transformation of Growing Healthy Churches will continue your explorations of inner space and find there your voice emboldened by God to prepare you for the inevitable violent shaking of the gap. May you find God's assurance in the depths of your heart for your own breaking of the sound barrier. And in the supersonic and stratospheric leap that follows, may you find the smooth air of ministry that allows us all to soar as we fly forward in fulfillment of Christ's Great Commission.

Meditations for the New Millennium

As a mighty wind

You swept over chaos
Before it was organized.

You wrestled with earth,
You struggled with water,
You battled with fire.

You kissed them
With your breath;
Life called from inertia.

We behold you in awe.

As a mighty wind
You sweep over order
And create chaos.

You wrestle with earth,
You struggle with water,
You battle with fire.

You crush life
With your breath;
And return all to chaos.

We behold you in fear.

Thou givest, and
Thou takest away.

As a mighty wind
Spirit sweeps through order and chaos alike,
By both, creating our human community;

Awed by life, assuaging fear,
Offering gratitude and grief,
Perspective and expectation.

We behold it in awe.

We give, and
We receive.[2]

NEXT STEP:
PACK YOUR PARACHUTE!

If you enjoyed *Women Married to Men in Ministry*, then get ready to Pack Your Parachute!

*P*ack Your Parachute is a combination day or weekend instruction/reflection retreat and ten-week guidebook/journal devotional. Choose one or both—they are designed expressly to equip and encourage women in ministry and Women Married to Men in Ministry. The wholistic set of topics covered by speaker/author/dramatist Teresa Flint-Borden includes:

1. Whole-person identity
2. Spirituality
3. Generations and legacies
4. Acceptance and forgiveness
5. Community and support
6. Purposeful living to contribute to society and kingdom
7. Education
8. Entertainment and leisure
9. Beauty inside and out
10. Spiritual renewal: love, hope, and faith

This isn't about selfish introspection, but lifesaving measures and being prepared for quality ministry. Whether you have just begun the journey to break the sound barrier or are soaring toward Mach-10 ministry, *Pack Your Parachute* is for you! Expect to learn and laugh in a safe environment. Find voice for your deepest needs and highest joys. And perhaps you'll be inspired, challenged, and maybe even a little relieved by dramatic performances of biblical women who were not so very different from ourselves. *Pack Your Parachute* will provide safe landings for Women Married to Men in Ministry.

QUESTIONS ABOUT SYSTEMIC CHANGE

The following questions were submitted to a panel of men and women in leadership of systemic change ministries. They hint at the range of everyday concerns leaders face in this process and demonstrate why *Women Married to Men in Ministry: Breaking the Sound Barrier Together* emphasizes the issues that it does.

General Concerns

- I would like your assistance and advice, as I am now in a leadership role for the first time. This position is very challenging, and I need to know how to handle the role and conduct myself. I feel neither competent nor confident in this role.
- Why do competent businesspeople leave their skills and education at the church door?
- We seem to be living in an entitlement culture that the churches have not escaped. We try to recognize people individually, personally, and professionally. We recognize marriages, birthdays, anniversaries, and it still seems not to be enough. What should I do to make people happy?
- What is Growing Healthy Churches doing to grow and at what cost?
- What have we done lately?
- What future events are possible?

- If you could choose only five key indicators for a healthy church, what would they be?
- What lessons can the church take for preventing a Katrina disaster regarding poor government response in decision-making?
- People have told me to "just be myself." I'm not sure how to do that within the Christian cultural environment.

Leadership in General

- Does the pastor have to be tough and callous in order to get results—is that really a win in the long run?
- What is the definition of *candor*? How can I know I am not being mean-spirited in my candor?
- There is so much beating around the bush and phoniness. What can I do to get to the heart of the issues?
- What is the real reason women can't seem to get ahead in church leadership? There still are not very many women pastors and fewer women in top leadership positions within the Christian realm.
- Everyone says it's important to find a good mentor, but I really don't know how to do that or what it means.
- My wife and I rarely see competence, but we do see very poor decision-making and outright un-Christian and unprofessional behavior within the Christian community where we work. Why is it so hard to find a leader we can respect, follow, and learn something from?

Change, Loss, Resistance

- Why is the church so resistant to change, or why do people feel that the church should not change?
- Is there a shortcut to the change process?
- What changes keep us up at night with worry?
- What do we need to stop doing?
- I know change is very important, but I also value relationships. Do they have to be sacrificed on the altar of change?
- I have been blindsided and backstabbed so many times by such unexpected people that I have a very low level of trust and have no one to talk to or confide in. I just feel like giving up.

- People I thought were my friends turned on both me and my spouse over an issue of change. It has been very painful, and, as a result, I feel betrayed.
- I have been leading systemic change in our church for a year with enormous growth prospects, but now I find myself facing a real barrier to this process and the progress we have made. There are members older than me and with more experience who have seen pastors come and go, and they are resistant and unwilling to change. It has stopped me in my tracks, and I have had to regroup for more than six months to get them to accept different ways of doing things. What should I do next?
- What is the process for building trust more quickly?

Staffing Issues

- What could possibly be more important than who gets hired, developed, promoted, and moved out the door? I feel very insecure with staffing issues. What can I do to learn these important skills better?
- My staff and volunteers are burning out, and I can't seem to find new leaders to fill the positions. The biggest challenge seems to be motivating people to the new vision. What can I do?
- How do I attract good staff and become a preferred church employer?

Family Matters

- What should I do to prepare for the change process that my husband is leading?
- How much church business/politics do I disclose to my wife? How can I protect my wife from the mean-spirited politicking of change within the church?
- My husband seems to keep everything to himself, and I feel like an outsider when it comes to church business and decisions that are made that will impact my life. I don't know what to do.

APPENDIX 3

RESOURCES

Assessment Tools and Self-Understanding

Bugbee, Bruce. *What You Do Best in the Body of Christ*. Grand Rapids: Zondervan, 1995.
Littauer, Florence. *Hope for Hurting Women*. Waco, Tex.: Word Book Publishers, 1985.
———. *Personality Plus: How to Understand Others by Understanding Yourself*. Tarrytown, N.Y.: F. H. Revell, 1992.
Myers Briggs Temperament Indicator (MBTI). DiSC Personality Profile. StrengthFinders (see Marcus Buckingham's book *Now, Discover Your Strengths*). Skills and spiritual gift inventories.

Marriage

Mathews, Alice, and M. Gay Hubbard. *Marriage Made in Eden: A Pre-Modern Perspective for a Post-Christian World*. Grand Rapids: Baker Books, 2004.

Change, Transition, and Transformation

Bridges, William. *Managing Transitions: Making the Most of Change*. Reading, Mass.: Addison-Wesley, 1991.
Duck, Jeanie Daniel. *Change Monster: The Human Forces That Fuel or Foil Corporate Transformation and Change*. New York: Crown Business, 2001.
Quinn, Robert E. *Deep Change: Discovering the Leader Within*. San Francisco: Jossey-Bass, 1996.
Southerland, Dan. *Transitioning: Leading Your Church Through Change*. Grand Rapids: Zondervan, 2000.

Spiritual and Personal Development

Books by Joyce Meyer can be found at www.JoyceMeyer.org and many other bookstores.
Books by Beth Moore can be found at www.cokesbury.com and many other bookstores.

Quinn, Janet F. *I Am a Woman Finding My Voice: Celebrating the Extraordinary Blessings of Being a Woman.* New York: Eagle Brook, 1999.

Relationships and Ministry

Frazee, Randy. *The Connecting Church.* Grand Rapids: Zondervan, 2001.
Mathews, Alice. *Preaching That Speaks to Women.* Grand Rapids: Baker Academic, 2002.

Inspiration and Personal Reflection

The Book of Common Prayer
Brazelton, Katie. *Conversations on Purpose for Women.* Grand Rapids: Zondervan, 2005.
———. *Pathway to Purpose for Women: Connecting Your To-Do List, Your Passions, and God's Purposes for Your Life.* Grand Rapids: Zondervan, 2005.
Campbell, Don. *The Roar of Silence: The Healing Powers of Breath, Tone, and Music.* Wheaton, Ill.: Quest Books, 1989.
Dillow, Linda. *The Blessing Book.* Colorado Springs: NavPress, 2003.
Goleman, Daniel. *Emotional Intelligence: Why It Can Matter More Than IQ.* New York: Bantam, 2006.
———. *Social Intelligence: The New Science of Human Relationships.* New York: Bantam, 2006.
Hart, Archibald D. *The Hidden Link Between Adrenaline and Stress.* Nashville: Thomas Nelson, 1995.
The Holy Bible
Lewis, C. S. *The Problem of Pain.* San Francisco: HarperSanFrancisco, 2004.
Maccaro, Janet. *Breaking the Grip of Dangerous Emotions.* Lake Mary, Fla.: Siloam Press, 2001.
Moore, Beth. *Praying God's Word: Breaking Free from Spiritual Strongholds.* Nashville: Broadman & Holman, 2000.
Ornish, Dean. *Love and Survival: The Scientific Basis for the Healing Power of Intimacy.* New York: HarperCollins, 1998.
Osterhaus, James P., Joseph M. Jurkowski, and Todd A. Hahn. *Thriving Through Ministry Conflict: By Understanding Your Red and Blue Zones.* Grand Rapids: Zondervan, 2005.
Oz, Mehmet. *Healing from the Heart.* New York: Dutton, 1998.
Rubin, Jordan. *The Maker's Diet.* Lake Mary, Fla.: Siloam Press, 2004.
Schlessinger, Laura. *Bad Childhood, Good Life: How to Blossom and Thrive in Spite of an Unhappy Childhood.* New York: HarperCollins, 2006.
Swenson, Richard A. *Margin: Restoring Emotional, Physical, Financial, and Time Reserves to Overloaded Lives.* Colorado Springs: NavPress, 2004.
Watson, Brenda. *The HOPE Formula: The Ultimate Health Secret.* Clearwater, Fla.: Renew Life Press, 2002.
———. *Gut Solutions.* Clearwater, Fla.: Renew Your Life Press, 2003.

————. *Renew Your Life: Improved Digestion and Detoxification*. Clearwater, Fla.: Renew *Life Press*, 2002.

Wiersbe, Warren W. *The Bumps Are What You Climb On: Encouragement for Difficult Days*. Grand Rapids: Baker Books, 1980.

Keep a personal Conversations with Jesus Journal.

Keep a personal Gratitude Journal.

Review the relaxation response technique at www.thebodysoulconnection.com/Educa tionCenter/index.htm.

Growing Healthy Churches Resources

Bennett, David. *The Get Out of Debt Club*. DVD 2006. Available through www.grow inghealthychurches.org.

Borden, Paul D. *Direct Hit*. Nashville: Abingdon Press, 2006.

————. *Hit the Bullseye*. Nashville: Abingdon Press, 2003.

Hoyt, William. *Effectiveness by the Numbers*. Nashville: Abingdon Press, 2007.

Jackson, John. *Learning Your Leadership Style*. Nashville: Abingdon Press, 2007.

Kaiser, John Edmund. *Winning on Purpose*. Nashville: Abingdon Press, 2006.

You may contact Teresa Flint-Borden at: www.growinghealthychurches.org or www.women-of-the-word.org.

Notes

Introduction

1. Women and Men are separate beings while still being dependent on each other (1 Corinthians 11:1-16). I hyphenate fe-male to emphasize her personal being while still recognizing the mutual interdependence.

1. Breaking the Sound Barrier

1. William Bridges, *Managing Transitions: Making the Most of Change* (Reading, Mass.: Addison-Wesley, 1991).
2. Robert E. Quinn, *Deep Change: Discovering the Leader Within* (San Francisco: Jossey-Bass, 1996).
3. W. Graham Scrooggle, *A Guide to the Gospels* (London: Pickering Linglis, 1965), 375.
4. Chuck Yeager, *An Autobiography* (New York: Bantam, 1986), 164.

2. Realities of Living in Systemic Change

1. Bryan Cutshall, *Where Are the Armorbearers: Strength and Support for Spiritual Leaders* (Cleveland, Tenn.: Pathway Press, 2005), 29-31.
2. James Belasco and Ralph Stayer, *Flight of the Buffalo: Soaring to Excellence, Learning to Let Employees Lead* (New York: Warner Books, 1993), 312.
3. Mort Orman, "7 Keys to Listening That Will Win You Friends, Improve Your Marriage, Boost Your Profits, and Make People Want to Follow You Anywhere." Online: www.stresscure.com/relation/7keys.html. Accessed June 30, 2007.

3. Journey through Time

1. Orville Wright, ed., *How We Invented the Airplane: An Illustrated History* (Mineola, N.Y.: Dover Books, 1988).
2. John F. Kennedy, "Address Before the Irish Parliament" (Dublin, June 28, 1963). Online: www.jfklibrary.org/Historical+Resources/Archives/Reference+Desk/Speeches/JFK/003POF03IrishParliament06281963.htm. Accessed July 1, 2007.

4. Flight Plan

1. Joe Aldrich, *Lifestyle Evangelism: Learning to Open Your Life to Those Around You* (Colorado Springs: Multnomah Books, 2006).
2. C. S. Lewis, *The Problem of Pain* (New York: HarperCollins, 1996), 91.

5. Getting Ready to Launch

1. Midrash Yalkut Shimoni, Beha'alotcha, 738.
2. This is why I am considering opening a Day Spa Retreat Center.

6. Voices Now and Then

1. Chris Glaser, *Communion of Life: Meditations for the New Millennium* (Louisville: Westminster John Knox Press, 1999), Day 14.
2. Don Campbell, *The Roar of Silence: The Healing Powers of Breath, Tone, and Music* (Wheaton, Ill.: Quest Books, 1989), 20.
3. Marge Piercy, "Unlearning to Not Speak" (Wellfleet, Mass.: Leapfrog Press).

7. Co-ministry Couples and Copiloting the Plane

1. "Mind the Gap: Space Scientists Uncover Causes of Gap in Van Allen Belts." Online: www.sciencedaily.com/releases/2006/09/060926171157.htm.
2. Lisa Takeuchi Cullen, "Pastors' Wives Come Together," March 29, 2007. Online: www.time.com/time/magazine/article/0,9171,1604902-2,00.html.
3. Ronald E. Keener, "Changing Role of the Pastor's Wife: Sometimes It Takes Possibility Thinking," *Church Executive* (April 2007). Online: www.churchexecutive.com/Page.cfm/PageID/8716. Accessed July 6, 2007.

8. Transformed through the Journey

1. Jean Baker Miller, *Toward a New Psychology of Women* (Boston: Beacon Press, 1976), 83, quoted in Carol Gilligan, *In a Different Voice: Psychological Theory and Women's Development* (Cambridge, Mass.: Harvard University Press, 1982), 169.
2. Gilligan, *In a Different Voice*, 171.
3. Ibid., 173.
4. Dane Rudhyar, "Dissonant Harmony: A New Principle of Musical and Social Organization." Online: www.khaldea.com/rudhyar/dissonantharmony.html. Accessed July 6, 2007.
5. Klyne Snodgrass, *Between Two Truths: Living with Biblical Tensions* (Grand Rapids: Zondervan, 1990), 32.
6. Brad Sargent, "Groundbreaking Concepts" (unpublished article, 2007).

9. Self-care for Success of Whole-person Copilots

1. Albert E. Brumley, "I'll Fly Away," from *Wonderful Message* (Hartford, Ark.: Hartford Music Co., 1932).

2. Don Colbert, *The Seven Pillars of Health* (Lake Mary, Fla.: Siloam Press, 2007), 30–35.

10. Flight Teams and a View from Space

1. See Appendix 3, Resources, in this book.

2. Chris Glaser, "Meditations for the New Millennium," *Communion of Life: Meditations for the New Millennium* (Louisville: Westminster John Knox, 1999), Day 38.

Chuck Yeager illus — p. 16f